Other books by Bernard Botein

THE PROSECUTOR
TRIAL JUDGE

BERNARD BOTEIN

AND

MURRAY A. GORDON

THE TRIAL

OF THE FUTURE:

Challenge to the Law

SIMON AND SCHUSTER

NEW YORK / 1963

CONTENTS

PREFACE

In February 1960, I delivered the nineteenth annual Benjamin N. Cardozo Lecture before the Association of the Bar of the City of New York. It bore the formidable title "The Future of the Judicial Process: Challenge and Response"; and from that lecture this book was hatched.

I pointed out that until recently the law could afford to respond at a deliberate pace to the problems created by slowly emerging social, political, technological and industrial change. But the flow of change has quickened and deepened. We can no longer cope with it in the same leisurely fashion. And, I might add, attempts to do so court acute danger to our society. A generation ago a car driven at the rate of thirty miles an hour could keep abreast of traffic; on a superhighway of today it would not only block progress but might prove a definite menace.

The Cardozo Lecture was addressed essentially to my coprofessionals of the bench and bar, as sentinels charged with a certain responsibility to the community who should be alive to the challenge of change. It sounded the alarm and recommended the establishment of an agency that would identify, analyze and advise on converging trends presaging problems for the world of law—which, of course, means problems for the world at large.

Friends who heard the lecture thought it contained the potential for a book addressed to a larger, more general audience. To meet the demands of such a volume, I enlisted the collaboration of Murray A. Gordon, a member of the New York bar. We hope we may have helped to stimulate the kind of public discussion which our society requires in order that law and lawyers may be able to meet the challenge of the changing world we live in.

BERNARD BOTEIN

CHAPTER ONE

THE LAW

ON AN AUGUST DAY in the year 1808 an Englishman named Forrester was making some repairs to his house. The house adjoined a road, and in the course of his task Forrester placed a pole on his side of the highway. At eight o'clock that evening, when house-holders were just beginning to light candles but while there was still enough light to afford visibility for a distance of a hundred yards, one Butterfield left a nearby tavern and mounted his horse. He came galloping at the breakneck speed of twelve miles an hour, rode violently against the pole, was thrown from his horse and sustained serious injuries.

In due course suit was instituted. The jurors were instructed that if Butterfield could have seen and avoided the obstruction by riding with reasonable and ordinary care they should find for the defendant, which they proceeded to do. The judgment was appealed. In 1809, in what has become the noted case of *Butterfield* v. *Forrester,* Lord Ellenborough enunciated the rule of contributory negligence, one of the most influential doctrines in the entire field of law, and one of the harshest in its application. The slightest lapse from ordinary care on the part of the plaintiff will completely bar recovery for his injuries, no matter how flagrant the negligence of the defendant may be.

The contributory negligence rule was part of a complex of law pronounced at the turn of the nineteenth century to help nurture the growth of infant industry. It was believed to be economically and politically essential to protect budding businesses by drastically limiting their liability for accidents. But the need, if it ever existed, has unquestionably long since vanished. Industry has become strongly established; all kinds of insurance coverage have developed. Modern machines have replaced the horse and buggy and hand loom, and accidents that had hatched at a leisurely enough pace to be avoided by exercise of reasonable prudence now happen in the flicker of an eyelid. Nevertheless, it was not until 1945 that the doctrine of contributory negligence was modified in England by legislation, and so-called comparative negligence statutes were enacted. Under the comparative negligence rule the negligence of the plaintiff no longer barred his recovery, but instead operated to reduce the recovery in proportion to the contributory negligence. The doctrine of contributory negligence, however, still prevails in all but a few of our states.

We explain later why legal precepts as harsh and unrealistic as that of contributory negligence are never abrogated promptly by judges, and seldom by legislators, even after their usefulness is spent. At this point we need only comment that the narrow dirt road on which Mr. Forrester left his pole has been replaced by multilaned, concrete highways, on which it is sometimes dangerous to drive an automobile at less than sixty miles an hour. In the atmosphere above jet planes speed by at the rate of hundreds of miles an hour. Rockets are shot into the stratosphere or into orbit in the ionosphere with incredible velocity that eludes the eye and defies the imagination. Yet in full view of all these manifestations of swift and radical change, the law still plods along on Mr. Butterfield's horse in most states of the Union.

Anticipating the foreseeable advances of science and technology, public agencies and private entrepreneurs plan enormous undertakings. Nations spend billions in research and experimentation to place the first man on the moon. Whole communities of vacation resorts are planned in reliance on improved methods of reclaiming hitherto unusable land, or on the future spread of better and easier means of transportation. Companies hoard huge reserve funds to replace machines that are not yet obsolete with equipment not yet designed, but which the march of events promises inexorably must soon be produced. As compared with only a few decades ago, the onrush of scientific and technological change is much too rapid for comfortable accommodation. Men in government, in business, in many small as well as large institutions can and do no longer wait until change is upon them to start planning and rebuilding, because the pace is so fast that those who wait are inundated by the remorseless, pounding waves of change.

But our men of law, with eyes to see and trained minds disciplined to thinking ahead, still ride Mr. Butterfield's horse on a narrow dirt road. Such archaism can be a wholesale societal drag, since the judicial process is charged with enforcing traffic regu-

lations for almost every aspect of the world's caval-
cade. It is because there is desperate need to revise
these regulations radically that this book is written.
Rules that were adequate in 1809 for a horse-drawn
society can be downright dangerous for a 1963 society
that would choke if confined to a narrow dirt road.

No responsible builder will set off an explosion
until he has taken every precaution to protect the
lives and property of people in the neighborhood.
Yet fuses have already been lit to a number of explosive charges that may twist the world of law out of
its present shape. Little, if anything, is being done
to protect that world against inevitable disruptions,
although the legal process, which is our social binding, threatens to burst its seams.

Of course, most people like to plan ahead comfortably with familiar materials toward familiar goals.
They regard the unfamiliar as the unlikely, and think
to hold back the inevitable by clinging to the immediate. In the field of law the tendency to avoid the
new and untried is more pronounced than in any
other calling. Delay itself is a prized technique of a
legal profession trained to digest change slowly.
Physicians should not write out prescriptions for
wonder drugs until lengthy experimentation has as-
sured them there will be no collateral effects. And
likewise judges will not write out decisions to resolve new problems until they are sure the nostrum
will not be worse than the problem it is designed to
cure. So the law deliberately grinds slow, in the hope
that it may grind sure; and deliberate delay, as opposed to indifferent procrastination, has become a
deeply ingrained professional reaction.

As will be demonstrated, the law could afford to

amble along at a leisurely rate when the traffic of world events also moved at a slow pace, because in good time the law would overtake events. With the speed at which currently shaping political, scientific, economic and social innovations hurtle by, there is no such assurance today. Unless the law bestirs itself, newly created conditions will be upon us too rapidly to be controlled effectively by legal ramparts hastily thrown together.

Ironically enough, lawyers who play so important a role in preparing meat packers, motion picture companies, oil producers and many other industries to cushion themselves against, or even capitalize upon, the velocity of scientific advance, rarely do as much for their own profession. Even so forward-looking a judicial statesman as Judge Cardozo did not think in terms of anticipating and forestalling future problems, but was content to await the impact of their arrival.

In his famous "Ministry of Justice" speech, delivered over forty years ago, Cardozo advocated an agency that could cope with problems besetting the courts, *after* "function is deranged." This process is called law revision. The law revision procedure operates in New York and other jurisdictions. It serves to clear the way, after study and consultation with judges, public officials, lawyers and others, for remedial legislation that will modify or eliminate existing defects and anachronisms in the courts. In New York a Law Revision Commission was interposed between court and legislature to point out the need for such legislation, because experience had proven that courts could not and legislatures did not make necessary changes of their own initiative. If

Cardozo's intelligence had been addressed to today's accelerated rate of change in the law, he would undoubtedly have recognized that upcoming legal obsolescence is no less critical than existing legal anachronism. And we suspect that he would have creatively wrought an institution for law prevision as well as law revision—to deal with anticipated as well as existing conditions. Cardozo may have suggested as much when he repeated the dictum of Maitland, the English legal historian, that "today we study the day before yesterday, in order that yesterday may not paralyze today, and today may not paralyze tomorrow."

The judicial process, which we see confronted by an unappraised future, is the law's center of gravity because it is the means by which courts decide cases. It is the method of resolving conflict peaceably by first finding out what happened and then enforcing the law applicable to the situation. Of course, the judicial process is more than just making and enforcing conflict-ending decisions. Clubs and, later, guns have accomplished and do accomplish this much. The object is to decide fairly and rationally, as well as effectively; and, just as important, to win the community's respect and approval, and satisfy its concepts of justice. The body of law which governs this judicial process comes from constitution, statute, and, more usually, what is known as the common law.

This common law, which has been developing since the thirteenth century in England, derives its name from the fact that it was a body of law common to all of England and not merely to one locality. Imported into the American colonies, it is now so firmly entrenched in this country that it is often called Anglo-American law. It has evolved through decisions handed down by many thousands of judges dealing with situations presented by actual cases. Sometimes judges have created new law to meet new problems. Sometimes they have refined old decisions to cope with old problems taking on new implications in a changing world. The common law is therefore a judge-made mosaic of closely meshed decisions, decisions possessing amazing uniformity even though each could pass directly only upon the specific problems posed by a particular lawsuit.

So it is understandable that the common law, with all its capacity to absorb and reflect change, advances slowly, rarely ever sweeping an entire body of outmoded or inefficient law into the discard. The fact that a legislature likewise seldom exercises this power of peaceful revolution attests to the vitality of the common law. Customs and traditions often govern behavior more effectively than written laws or codes. Where customs and traditions have lost acceptance, laws cannot be hurled into the breach as a substitute.

One of the dividends of the slow march of the law has been that the seasonal problems arising from short-lived public impulses tend to die off or to decide themselves. There are left the hard, persistent questions on which the constant yet adaptable principles of common law have been and will continue to be refined. We suspect that this marking of time has not been altogether unpremeditated.

Today and tomorrow, however, the law's slow pace of the past would be intolerable. Many swift, radical changes already here or just around the corner can no longer be digested by the law without acute distress.

Barbara Ward put it accurately when she told us recently that "As the world enters the Nineteen Sixties one fact seems sure. The pace of revolutionary change in every sphere of human affairs will gather momentum." The telescoping within a short period of time of a quick succession of scientific miracles, of accelerated social and political changes, has brought about critical wrenches in our way of life; and a heightened receptivity to change is abroad today. We can no longer hope that these changes will settle in so gradually that the conventional techniques of the judicial process will be permitted their own leisurely and after-the-fact accommodations without intervening periods of embarrassing futility.

The alarm must not be sounded just for the legal profession alone. The interrelationships among clients, lawyers, judges and jurors—potentially the entire population—in the functioning of the judicial process attest that it is a proper concern of all of us. The trial process, from a traffic court case to the gravest homicide prosecution, involves everyone as participant or public.

Ultimately, all law begins and all law ends with the man in the street. At the least his needs, and at the most his faith, are communicated to judges and legislators and heighten their sense of accountability. They must heed his voice, because in essence they merely bring their expertness to bear upon his notions of justice and values. But the man in the street will raise his voice only at rare intervals, only when his sense of security is threatened because the values he expects his system of law to safeguard are endangered. The result is that public as well as profession moves to meet change only when obsolescence has set in to the point of crisis or traumatic injustice. Too frequently a cautious profession and not an apathetic public is then blamed, particularly as the time lag inherent in juridical change often gives unjustified basis for the popular feeling that the lawyers' disciplined sense of justice has atrophied their sense of indignation. The onrushing dilemma for the judicial process will be to retain the indispensable respect and confidence of the public by shortening the time lag, while still exercising deliberative judgment—this in the face of explosive changes which are happening, as Robert Heilbroner has observed, "in a time so compressed . . . that it is as if huge seismic slippages were occurring in the deepest substratum of history."

Nearly all meaningful changes faced by modern society are already producing difficult cases in the courts. For change has not been confined to science, industry and technology. It has curved away from the laboratory to the home, the job and the family, and, as will be detailed in succeeding chapters, must inevitably lodge in the courts and there dislodge some of the most cherished attributes of our legal system.

Just a few examples:

Donald L. Michael of the Peace Research Institute has said that "cybernation presages changes in the social system so vast and so different from those with which we have traditionally wrestled that it will challenge to their roots our current perceptions about the viability of our way of life." Thus, the use of computers in absorbing and cataloging evidence in any one case or in a run of factually related cases may make our present notions of thorough preparation for trial seem puerile, and may extend to a variety of judgments now committed to the jury. The genius of the Anglo-American system of law lies in the fact that the liberty of most persons involved in its processes is ultimately committed to the care of their peers. Will this solicitude for individual rights and dignity dwindle if, in many substantial respects, a machine rather than his peers passes in judgment on a party's rights?

Future electronic, psychoanalytical and narcoanalytical techniques for inducing recall and disclosures of past events may prove much more dependable and truth-productive than our highly prized testimonial processes, cross-examination and all. Our traditional ground rules are designed to elicit truth on the notion that justice will follow truth. But what if scientific intrusions upon the unconscious can reproduce truth more reliably and effectively than does our present system of presentation of proof? If so, there will then be posed the fundamental threshold question as to whether witnesses may be compelled to submit to such procedure, which entails invasion of privacy and freedom of will.

New notions of leisure values are developing rapidly. We have not yet attained the full status of a so-called leisure society, but even now large portions of our population are for the first time enjoying and setting great store by their leisure hours. It is not too early to begin to contemplate seriously the upcoming need for the judicial process to deal with hitherto unrecognized leisure values of privacy, beauty and fun.

Another example: the family has felt the accumulated impact of all the change produced by auto and airplane, mass media of communication, the social revolution in morals and manners and the technology which has produced mechanical refrigeration in the home and other labor-saving home appliances. Our laws and mores concerning sex shift uncertainly from Pollyanna to Peyton Place, with an occasional taking of inventory by Kinsey. Our courts, serving as society's forum for resolving the radical changes resulting from such instability, must expect an increasing volume and variety of family problems, requiring new techniques for their accommodation. Even now, conflict in the home and neglect of the young are regarded as matters of community concern and not as partisan private brawls or tragedies to be left in the courts to the fortuitous justice of the ordinary adversary procedure. In this area the judicial process is avowedly beginning to look for solutions on a societal basis, rather than in conventional judicial judgments for or against one of the parties involved. Such a transition from a court of judgment to a court of therapy will carry in its wake great consequences to a lawyer-dominated adversary system traditionally associated with due process in trials. How then will the new court and the old values of due process be accommodated, if at all?

From these few examples it must be evident that likely changes in our judicial process are as profound as they are limitless. The need to anticipate such changes as can be reasonably projected into the future is especially urgent in the world of law. We simply cannot continue to graft onto our legal structure changes that are usually unplanned and just echoes of other institutional transformations. We dare say that in no other aspect of our society is the need to interest the public and inform it of the shape of things to come so importunate as in the judicial process. Any of the developing patterns may emerge as boon or specter from the womb of the judicial process. But as it is apparent that stretching existing doctrine to cover newly emerging values will cruelly test the law's tensile strength, we should start now to draw judicial blueprints for the future.

Where change is explosive by reason of its speed and magnitude, intelligent anticipation is the only alternative to chaos. We believe this is pertinent to the judicial process as well as to other less encrusted institutions. It is timely to construct the machinery of anticipation necessary to enable that process to avoid the obsolescence which is today measured by years rather than by centuries. We do not thereby merely discount at present rates the problems of the future; we also illumine the problems of the present, for, as John Dewey remarked, "thought about future happenings is the only way we can judge the present; it is the only way to appraise its significance."

CHAPTER TWO

THE TRIAL

MEN OF LAW have progressed far beyond their barbaric ancestors in the application of truth-finding procedures, just as the modern physician has advanced beyond the tribal medicine man in diagnosis and cure. Yet the road has been slow. The law must admit newly proposed trial techniques slowly and carefully lest in strengthening one element of the trial complex it destroy another jealously guarded prerogative. New ways of establishing the truth may, and frequently do, intrude dangerously on traditional rights. And so the trial process—our method for determining the facts upon which judicial decision is based—is continuously involved, among other things, in balancing efficient fact-finding techniques with the individual and social values and rights threatened by those techniques.

This apprehension that a new fact-finding process might disturb settled procedures usually creates a considerable time lag between its acceptance by the scientific world and its approval by the legal world. In addition, change-resistant inertia, plus the tendency to venerate traditional trial techniques long after their claim to superior validity in truth-finding has been forfeited, lengthens this period. The span between the discovery and the judicial application of new fact-finding devices necessarily imposes a heavy, often agonizing, penalty on those who, in the interim, may have been denied justice because of the unavailability of those devices. But as new and particularly convincing methods for finding the truth in disputed issues emerge on the scientific horizon, they will surely produce urgent and inescapable problems. We are presently dragging in our consideration of those recent developments; and the rush of speed with which they come upon us makes it critically appropriate that we look toward and not away from them.

For centuries we have paid an exorbitant social penalty for failing to consider available fact-finding techniques with an appropriate sense of urgency. It must be remembered that although the Greeks and the Romans had developed a rational system of proof, nevertheless trial by ordeal of fire or water, compurgation and battle endured in Saxon and old English law until the thirteenth century; indeed, as late as 1818 wager of battle was claimed in England by a man charged with murder, leading finally to the formal abolition of that exotic piece of obsolescence. For almost two hundred years after the Norman Conquest, the defendant in English courts could continue to defeat a claim or charge levelled against him by obtaining a required number of other persons, known as compurgators, who would back his sworn denial by their own oaths. They swore to their belief in the truth of the assertions of the party for whom they vouched—that he did not owe the debt claimed, or that he was not guilty—upon their faith in the man, irrespective of whether they knew anything about the facts in controversy. If the party could not secure the specified number of compurgators, or if they did not swear in proper form, the "oath burst" and he lost. If he could produce the minimal number of properly sworn compurgators, he won. The sanction was a belief that if a compurgator swore falsely he would be punished from on high.

Until the Church in 1215 forbade the clergy to participate in the ritual of ordeals, English courts likewise continued after the Norman Conquest to employ trial by ordeal. This method of trial rested on the belief that, if properly invoked, God would intervene by sign or miracle to reveal the truth respecting the dispute between two contending parties. In the water ordeal, which was used for common folk, the accused plunged his hand into a cauldron of boiling water. After he withdrew it, the hand would be wrapped in cloths and the wrapping officially sealed by the judge or priest presiding at the ceremony. When three days had elapsed the cloths were removed. If the wound was clean, the accused was found innocent; if unclean, he was adjudged guilty. In the fire ordeal, which was confined to persons of higher rank, the test of innocence required the accused to carry a red-hot iron with his bare hand or to walk through fire or upon nine hot plowshares in his bare feet.

Upon the abolition of trial by ordeal, it was superseded by trial by combat. Parties and their witnesses could defend their cause and their veracity by combat, and a person could in this manner prove his innocence of crime or his right to property or money by physical prowess. Even the judge might be challenged to defend his judgment in such fashion. Only specified classes of persons, such as infants, women, or men over sixty years of age, could decline the battle; or they could designate champions to do battle on their behalf. Professional warriors roamed the country, ready to fight with weapons for litigants who retained them, much as circuit lawyers later fought with words.

The abandonment of ritualistic forms of trial did not bring promptly in their wake the trial process that we know today. By the thirteenth century trial by jury had replaced the medieval form of criminal trial, but a long time was to elapse before jurors would hear evidence. The members of the early jury were more in the nature of witnesses, rather than judges of the facts as we know them today. As we point out later, the jury was first established after the Norman Conquest as a reconnaissance system for the benefit of the Norman invaders. As the jury system was extended to the trial of issues of fact, the jury continued to be selected from neighbors who personally knew something about the situation in dispute. In effect, the consequences of the oath shifted from the party or his compurgators to the jurors, who would render their verdict on the knowledge of the case they had garnered prior to trial. Not until the fifteenth century was the jury's knowledge of the facts enlarged by the evidence of witnesses, and not until the early part of the eighteenth century were the functions of witness and juror finally and formally severed from each other. Yet, many centuries earlier the Greeks and Romans had developed a trial procedure based on evidence by witnesses.

The tenacity of older forms in the trial process is also illustrated by the astounding circumstance that in England, until the last century, parties to a law-

suit, their husbands and wives, even any person having a financial interest in the outcome, were disqualified from taking the witness stand. The basis
for this exclusion was the fear that such persons were
very likely to testify falsely to protect their own
interests. Imagine trying a case today in which the
plaintiff, defendant and all witnesses financially interested—often the only ones who know anything
about the case—were not allowed to testify!

The parade of anachronisms could be extended far
into the darkness which is produced by unreasoned
resistance to change. It will suffice perhaps to mention
that as late as the nineteenth century the number of
evident absurdities in the trial process was sufficiently
great to engage a major part of the efforts of the
leading English reformer, Jeremy Bentham, and to
stock novels by Charles Dickens with objects of satire.
The consistent reluctance of the trial process—presumably dedicated to finding facts—to adopt available
techniques for finding such facts dictates a close, hard
look now at the trial process in the light of present
and likely advances of science in matters of fact-
finding.

The Anglo-American system of law currently pins
its faith on its adversary method. Each side, out of
self-interest, is expected to endeavor to bolster its
own version of the case and to demolish its oppon-
ent's contentions. The adversary method holds that
in the ensuing courtroom scrimmages the right will
prevail. Rules of law have been molded to fortify
this confidence that the stronger case will win.

Basic to the Anglo-American adversary trial process
is the faith reposed in cross-examination as an instrument for the revelation of truth. Many exclusionary

rules of evidence, such as the rule against hearsay, developed because the testimony involved was incapable of being tested by cross-examination. If a witness testified that Jones told him he saw the plaintiff lend money to the defendant, the latter could not cross-examine Jones under oath to test the truth of his statement; therefore Jones's statement would be excluded as hearsay. In similar vein, dangerous areas of proof which lend themselves to easy fabrication, such as certain transactions with dead persons, are forbidden. By confining evidence to those precincts which experience and logic have proved to be "safe" and fairly amenable to testing by cross-examination, the litigation process on the whole achieved excellent results; and its most buoyant votaries ascribe to it the qualities of a science. Judge Cardozo has said, however, that rules of evidence "have their source very often in considerations of administrative experience, of practical expediency and not in rules of logic."

Certainly the law of evidence has not been reduced to an exact science. A skillful perjurer will still confound a poor lawyer, and often prove a match for a good one. And a shrewd lawyer can often make an honest but dull-witted witness look like a perjurer. Such conscious perjury or manipulation of evidence is difficult enough to detect or expose. We are now also aware that many honest, well-intentioned witnesses will testify erroneously because of the defective functioning of their processes of perception, recollection or narration.

Hugo Munsterberg, more than a generation ago, described two so-called tableau experiments. They were conducted to test the reliability of original observation of an incident and the ability to remember and relate what happened, when the witnesses had every incentive to tell the truth. In one test, two students, by careful prearrangement, staged a quarrel and scuffle in a criminology class, during which a revolver went off. After the episode the professor asked some students for written reports, others for oral statements. The ratio of mistakes—consisting of material omissions, alterations and erroneous additions—ranged from 26 percent to 80 percent.

The other incident, also unexpected and startling, was staged before a meeting of a scientific body of trained observers—jurists, psychologists and physicians. A clown from a neighboring carnival burst into the meeting room, followed by a man with a revolver in his hand. Again, there was a large degree of error, by trained experts, in reporting the essential acts of the two men staging the tableau.

For a long time science has been deflating our notions about the infallibility of the trial process. More recently, the technicians have gone even further. There have been developed startling, effective techniques for "eavesdropping on man's unconscious," as it has been termed. If these techniques fulfill the expectations of many sober-minded men of science, the laboratory will be equipped to reveal truth much more efficiently and inexorably than the courtroom. We may reach the point where our present methods of resolving legal disputes may seem as archaic and barbaric as trial by ordeal seems to us today; and courtroom procedures as we know them may have to be scrapped.

Because we stand at the threshold of such a possibility, it should be profitable to review briefly the progress of science in the ascertainment of truth and to consider its implications for the administration of law in this country. If science can reproduce truth more reliably and effectively than our present system, we shall not be able long to defer our rendezvous with progress. The judicial test for admitting the fruits of scientific research is whether they have won general acceptance in the appropriate discipline. Because of this stringent test various newer truth-revealing techniques have not yet won admittance to the courthouse, but they are storming its steps.

In little more than half a century we have traveled, in our still-frightening interventions into the privacy of the mind, from Freud to brainwashing to subliminal projection—all encompassed within the notion that the operations and motivations of our mental processes are knowable, controllable, and even exploitable. In his *Brave New World Revisited,* Aldous Huxley is understandably appalled at the extent to which his fantasies of more than twenty-five years ago have been realized in modern manipulation of minds and emotions; George Orwell would be only a little less troubled at the prospect that in this aspect "1984" may be reached before that date. It is certain that by means of psychoanalytical, narcoanalytical and electronic techniques and devices, motivational research and chemistry, we shall attain greater insight into and control over the billions of units comprising the human brain. This rapidly advancing frontier that is being staked out amidst the mysteries of the mind augurs revolutionary changes in the trial process.

Fact-finding for trial purposes today depends in large measure upon articulate, communicable testimony reflecting the recollection of witnesses. As indicated, limitations of conscious memory, even aside from the distorting factors of self-interest and partisanship, make this process painfully fallible; and its deficiencies often cannot be cured by cross-examination, that revered rectifier of purposeful fabrication or unwitting error. And many times, even when recollection is accurate, tense and frightened witnesses fail to communicate accurately to judge or jury.

Recent experience with drugs such as scopolamine and the barbiturates (sodium pentothal and sodium amytal), techniques such as hypnosis and devices such as the lie detector should be, accordingly, of profound significance in our current trial procedures. These devices suggest the eventual emergence of scientifically accepted procedures for inducing the full and truthful recollection and the relaxed narration of events. The present unperfected nature of these fact-finding interventions, the circumstance that they are not uniformly operative and that some persons are able to lie or withhold information, form no basis for blinking the problems promised by their ultimate development.

Narcoanalysis, a term loosely blanketing procedures for interrogating subjects while they are in a state of partial unconsciousness induced by drugs, is the most dramatic of the techniques mentioned. The drugs employed in narcoanalysis serve as central nervous system depressants and thereby lessen inhibitions and other blocks to disclosures. The relationship between self-revelation and depressants of the central nervous system is not a novel discovery. The ancients recognized *in vino veritas,* as does any high school senior who has taken a forbidden swig from a flask. Primitive societies have long been familiar with the self-disclosure flowing from the use of drugs such as peyote, opium and canabis. It is no coincidence that Thomas de Quincey's *Confessions of an English Opium-Eater* has been designated by J. B. Priestley as "a masterpiece of *actual* autobiography," as well as of daydream and fantasy.

It remained, however, for modern man to put the revelatory by-products of cerebral depressants to systematic and organized use. In the late nineteenth century the latch was lifted by the application of hypnosis to the study of individual personality and of personality disorder. It was reported in 1893 that the Dutch had, by law, authorized the use of hypnotism in police investigation. This sequence is typical. The main aspiration of the scientist is to apply the revelations and relaxations of narcoanalysis to diagnosis and therapy; but its truth-divulging properties may also make it a significant instrument in the administration of justice. No doubt many scientists look at this tributary use as suspiciously as others view the use of nuclear energy for war purposes.

In the United States the importation of drug-induced disclosures into criminology was initiated by Dr. Robert E. House, an enterprising medical practitioner from Ferris, Texas. He had observed the amazingly candid and uninhibited remarks of women giving birth under the influence of scopolamine as an anesthetic—then known as the "twilight sleep" drug. Reasoning logically enough that a similar technique could be used in criminal investigation, he administered scopolamine in 1922 to establish the innocence of two convicted criminals and subsequently published his findings in a regional medical journal.

Later Dr. House employed scopolamine in the interrogation of at least eighty-four criminals or suspects, and then proceeded to expand his claimed discovery to the point of erroneously but euphemistically entitling the drug a "truth serum."

Understandably, various investigatory agencies have availed themselves of this technique for dragging the pool of man's unconscious. As far back as 1924 the district attorney of Birmingham, Alabama, used scopolamine to obtain confessions to twenty-five ax-murders from five suspects. For several decades the Scientific Crime Detection Laboratory of Northwestern University experimented with the same drug. So-called truth serum techniques have been used frequently by investigators of the Kansas City Police Department, by the University of Minnesota and by Dr. W. F. Lorenz at the University of Wisconsin. In June 1946, the press widely publicized the case of William Heirens, a seventeen-year-old murder suspect who feigned amnesia. He was interrogated while under the influence of sodium pentothal and confessed to three murders and more than five hundred burglaries.

The most extensive utilization of drugs to induce revelations occurred during World War II and, again, during the Korean War. Barbiturates were used in the psychiatric treatment of men suffering from battle shock or shell shock, who had developed amnesia, paralysis or other war neuroses. The drugs unloosed the soldier's account of the traumatic experience that had triggered his state of shock, serving to expedite and give direction to treatment.

Under the interpretation of The Hague and Geneva Conventions of War, drugs were apparently not used to any appreciable degree in the interrogation of prisoners of war. But sodium pentothal was employed by court-appointed psychiatrists in their questioning of Raymond Cens, placed on trial in France in 1948 as a Nazi collaborator, when he claimed to be suffering from aphasia. He did not oppose their use of the drug, but did object to their testimony as to the results of the test and, of course, their opinion that he was feigning aphasia. Following his conviction, he brought a civil action against the psychiatrists, charging assault and battery and violation of professional secrets. The suit was unsuccessful, but produced considerable discussion and a large body of literature on the subject in Europe. The Paris Bar Association criticized the psychiatrists on various grounds, one of them that Cens had been artificially deprived of his free will. Subsequently, in 1950, the Egyptian delegate to the United Nations offered a resolution, without success, for the inclusion in the Covenant on Human Rights of a prohibition against the use of "truth serum."

At the present writing, a confession made under the influence of a drug would appear to be judicially inadmissible in this country, on the ground that it was made involuntarily. In the well-known *Leyra* case, the New York Court of Appeals in 1951 held inadmissible a defendant's confession of the brutal murder of his aged parents where his confession was obtained during questioning by a psychiatrist practicing hypnosis. The current limitation upon the admissibility of statements made during an induced lapse of consciousness extends, however, beyond unwilling or incriminating disclosures. The courts generally also bar exonerating utterances resulting from voluntary submission to hypnosis or chemical depressants of the central nervous system. Apparently neither the conscious assent of the accused to the use of these novel procedures nor his exculpation by such procedures while conscious will serve to lift the current judicial barriers to statements made under the influence of narcoanalysis. In 1951 the California courts refused a defendant's request for his own interrogation under sodium pentothal; and statements of innocence made under drugs or hypnosis have been denied admission in evidence in North Dakota, Virginia, Missouri, California and Oklahoma.

The present skeptical judicial attitude toward the admissibility of drug-induced revelations is, no doubt, based largely upon the judiciary's uncertainty as to the reliability of the information thus obtained. In a 1960 decision excluding a drug-induced statement, a Kentucky judge colorfully held that he was "not disposed to lead a safari into that jungle without first being satisfied that the new devices . . . have attained full scientific acceptance." Many interviewees are not satisfactory subjects, even under ideal circumstances. Even good subjects are extremely suggestible while under the influence of drugs, and others, for neurotic or unconscious reasons, use the occasion to confess to crimes and other wrongdoings never perpetrated by them. On the other hand, some are able to withhold information and some to lie while under the influence of the drugs. Workers in the field report a heavy incidence of fantasy in the material produced, and it seems agreed that at this time, even for use outside the courts, the examinations must be conducted and the results interpreted only by experts in this field.

The camel's nose, however, is inside the judicial tent. At least one court at the trial level, in Wisconsin, has, upon the insistence of the defendant in a criminal case, admitted in evidence his version of the facts in issue resulting from his examination while under the influence of sodium amytal. More recently, in 1959, a federal trial court accepted a confession obtained from the defendant while he was intoxicated by demerol administered to relieve pain. As a general proposition, however, this type of evidence is reserved for the limited although very important purpose of proving sanity or insanity, or ability or inability to stand trial, rather than as bearing on whether the defendant committed the crime charged. In 1942, the New York Court of Appeals, in *People* v. *Esposito,* upheld the admissibility of psychiatric testimony that the defendants were sane and malingering in their claim of insanity where the testimony was based, in part, upon reactions of the defendants and information obtained from them after they had been injected with metrazol and sodium amytal. And, in 1959, the same court, in *People* v. *Higgins,* permitted testimony of psychiatrists, based in part upon an interview with the defendant while he was under the influence of sodium amytal, that in their opinion the defendant was in the throes of an epileptic fit when he committed the murder for which he was being prosecuted.

The slow and limited judicial acceptance of drug-induced revelations must be viewed in the light of similar judicial skepticism which existed and was ultimately dispelled by scientific progress leading eventually to court acceptance of fingerprint evidence, blood tests, and handwriting, X-ray and psychiatric testimony. Thus, although there has been a fairly consistent body of law rejecting findings from lie detector tests, the results of such a test were recently admitted in a New York case where the trial judge believed experience had established a sufficient foundation to validate the use of the machine. In the celebrated Alger Hiss trial, a psychiatrist employed by the defense observed the government's chief witness, Whittaker Chambers, on the witness stand. He was then permitted to give his opinion concerning Chambers' credibility, testifying that he was a psychopathic personality "with a tendency towards making false accusations."

It has been aptly said by a federal court in the leading case of *Frye* v. *United States* that "just when a scientific principle or discovery crosses the line between the experimental and demonstrable stages is difficult to define. Somewhere in this twilight zone the evidential force of the principle must be recognized . . ." The likely timetable of judicial acceptance of drug-induced disclosures will, no doubt, reflect the observation of our outstanding authority on the law of evidence, the late Professor Wigmore: "If there is ever devised a psychological test for the evaluation of witnesses, the law will run to meet it. . . . Whenever the psychologist is ready for the courts, the courts are ready for him."

In short, recent and probable future advances in the technique of inducing revelations by narcoanalysis and the general judicial receptivity to scientifically validated evidence remove this subject from the realm of science-fiction fantasy and dictate a sober consideration of the consequences to the judicial process.

These consequences hold implications for the administration of justice in this country far beyond the limited question of whether the laboratory technique will prove more efficient a fact-finder than our present practice. This relatively narrow question will soon be decided for us empirically by science. It is not sufficient merely to speculate whether, or even when, black judicial robes will be replaced with white laboratory smocks, or the arm upraised for the administration of the oath will be replaced with the arm extended for the administration of a hypodermic. For as drug-induced revelations gain acceptance in the determination of ultimate issues of innocence or guilt, the functions of the jury, judge and counsel will be profoundly affected. What will bedevil the legal profession are the social and political derangements that would follow in the wake of laboratory-sealed, guaranteed findings of fact and of truth. And in the litigation process such unavailable truths can work havoc with community values.

For example, in a criminal case the jury is expected to bring the compassion of the community into the courtroom. If the jury feels that a law designed to regulate human conduct in general is too harsh in the circumstances of a particular case, that jury will disregard impregnable factual evidence of guilt and return a verdict of not guilty. Indeed, just this characteristic of the jury in the 1735 acquittal of John Peter Zenger in New York contributed to the inclusion of the right to a jury trial in the Fifth Amendment to the United States Constitution.

Zenger, as editor of a weekly newspaper, criticized Colonial Governor William Crosby. Zenger was arrested and brought to trial on a charge of criminal libel before a judge who had been hand-picked by

Crosby for the palpable purpose of convicting the editor. Upon the trial, this judge instructed the jury that the published matter was libelous and that truth was no defense. Since Zenger admitted publishing the statements, this was tantamount to directing the jury to return a verdict of guilty. Nevertheless, Zenger's lawyer asked the jury to consider the truth of the alleged libel, and the jury returned a verdict of not guilty in the teeth of the judge's charge. Truth is now accepted in courts of law as a defense to libel charges.

To this day it is supposed that the jury serves as a merciful, albeit at times lawless, element in the daily administration of the law. Those who owe acquittals to the defense of the "unwritten law" are gratefully aware of the jury's capacity to legislate interstitially by subordinating a general principle of law to the equities of an individual case. There will be no room for such an escape valve if a group of scientists hands up a neatly packaged set of findings that indisputably show a violation of law.

Nor will the jury as easily be able to continue to serve as a sort of sounding board to indicate, by its refusal to convict on a showing of technical lawbreaking, that a certain law is unpalatable to the community. Jurors reflect the community; and it is healthy for legislators to know that the laws they pass must square with the jury's notions of fair play before they will be enforced.

In other areas of litigation there are laws in conflict with prevailing mores which are made endurable only because bench, bar and public have become conditioned to regard manifest fiction as expedient fact. Such laws, as Thurman Arnold pointed out, "survive in order to satisfy moral objections to established modes of conduct . . . [but] are unenforced because we want to continue our conduct, and are unrepealed because we want to preserve our morals." Judges have come to accept as truth the most incredible evidence of adultery in undefended divorce cases, even though the testimony has been tailored, in almost ritualistic language, to the requirements of the law by two spouses striving desperately to be rid of each other. If all witnesses in matrimonial matters testified under the influence of some reliable truth-revealing medium, there would be fewer dissolutions of marriage in states like New York, which on the face of their laws, at least, impose rigorous requirements.

Another area in which jurors deliberately disregard the letter of the law is in refusing to apply the previously mentioned rule of contributory negligence in present-day accident cases. In many accidents, and particularly in the vast number of motor vehicle collision cases, the plaintiff is guilty of some small degree of negligence. Understandably, the jury will not send him empty-handed from the courtroom if his negligence was comparatively less gross than the defendant's.

But the problems involved in accommodating the awful truth to unpalatable law will be only a small and comparatively simple part of the complex of adjustments that may have to be made. If we cross the threshold issue of the admissibility of data elicited by narcoanalysis, hovering beyond are the other consequences to the entire trial process resulting from the production of truth through means other than the conventional interrogation of witnesses by counsel. If through narcoanalysis witnesses can be depended upon to give truthful testimony, as they recall the events, will there be need for cross-examination? The entire adversary system of litigation may find its focus shifted from deciding conflicting evidence by the testimonial process inside the courtroom to scrutinizing the fairness and competency of the narcoanalytical process which produces the conclusive and uncontroverted facts, usually outside the courtroom.

There is no disposition to minimize the importance of insuring complete fairness in the methods by which such out-of-court evidence will be elicited. If anything, future advances in this area will make due process even more critical and essential than it is today. It has been charged that the Nazi and Communist regimes have "brainwashed" their victims so effectively that they have confessed to crimes they never committed, and implicated others who were wholly innocent.

Raymond Laporte, a French consul general in New York, who studied this problem as a result of his experience as a diplomat in Communist countries, has said:

> In the end, it is a question of perfecting a science which could be called "psychosynthesis" in opposition to psychoanalysis. Psychoanalysis consists of finding out the complexes of a given individual and curing him of them. "Psychosynthesis," on the contrary, consits of giving a person who has no complexes the complex of guilt.
>
> The methods used to obtain this result, this "conditioning" as Huxley would say, are well known today. They are based on psychological persuasion and taking advantage of the diminished intellectual

and mental resistance of the subject, conditioned by a concurrent rupture of the natural rhythms. For this method it is essential to isolate the subject totally from his normal environment and persons whom he knows. Between arrest and appearance before his judge, the accused should have no contact whatsoever except with those charged with "conditioning" him.

The risk of the development of some procedure akin to "psychosynthesis," even when administered in a good-faith search for truth rather than to impose a complexion of guilt on an innocent person, suggests the urgency of suitable safeguards. The courtroom thus shifts from a fact-finding forum to an instrument for testing the fairness of the extra-judicial fact-finding. Something of an historical antecedent to such a shift in judicial function is reflected in the rise of administrative agencies and arbitration tribunals to handle business that was formerly the subject of court litigation. Since these newly emerging tribunals did not inspire the same confidence as their traditional forbears, the courts were delegated to pass upon the propriety of the procedures employed by such agencies in the disposition of matters that had previously been within the jurisdiction of the courts.

As the novel methods of proof we have discussed assume greater scientific validity, serious questions must also arise as to whether findings of fact, of intention or of motive can be left, as now, to the nonscientific community of judges or juries, or whether that function will be for those whose special skills and training more particularly qualify them to appraise the materials resulting from such methods. Indeed, there would no doubt be agitation for the elimination of judge, jury and courtroom, as we know them, in favor of the more clinical precincts of the technician. Certainly, there would be a significant change in the roles presently played by courtroom principals; and this, too, can find parallels in the past. Max Radin has written that in Rome in the fourth and fifth centuries B.C., the initiative for truth-finding reposed in the judge. With the advent of the adversary, self-help form of litigation as we know it, which is usually waged through the opposing parties' lawyers, the judge's function evolved to what it is today, that of an umpire. It is not at all unlikely that the onus of motoring the fact-finding processes will shift from the lawyer to the scientist.

More subtle than the scuttling of the traditional trial process, but probably more critical in its societal implications, would be the effect of truth-revealing techniques on rights of the individual which have long been cherished and associated with protection of his person and dignity. We shall be unable to avoid re-examining the present practice of imposing upon the claimant in a civil action the burden of proving his version by a fair preponderance of the evidence, or requiring the prosecution in a criminal case to prove the defendant guilty beyond a reasonable doubt. The trial process is usually weighted on the side of the defending party. The law places a heavy burden on the complaining party who would enlist its resources to obtain relief. This is particularly true in criminal cases, where society seeks to balance the uneven resources of government and the accused individual so as to protect him from tyrants and powerful masters who possess the means to employ the courts as instruments of oppression.

But what need will remain for such weighting and protective rules, it will be argued, if the management of litigation by the parties themselves becomes minimal? Constitutional and common law safeguards, such as the provisions against self-incrimination, the presumption of innocence, the right to due process, are all commonly believed to be for the protection of the innocent. Again, what need in law or logic for invoking these protections when science can reliably establish such innocence without them? The language of the late United States Supreme Court Justice Jackson in *Stein* v. *New York* will be quoted for the proposition that constitutional doctrines are "not mere technical loopholes for the escape of the guilty."

A public trial, by jury in most instances, is another such highly regarded right. What need will there be for such a trial, it will no doubt be argued, when the determinative fact-finding will be transferred from the courtroom to the laboratory? Yet one must wonder how readily the bar and public will accept the resolution of legal controversies by technicians in the arcane seclusion of the laboratory instead of by judge or jury in the open courtroom.

It will be contended that since the end to be attained by the provisions of constitutional and common law is protection of the innocent, and since science will accomplish this so much more effectively than all of the legal doctrines laid end to end, *ergo,* this is one end that justifies the means. In such a view the presumption of innocence would be dissolved because it would become unnecessary. Likewise, a major justification for asserting the right against self-incrimination—that the innocent might become entangled in the toils of the law through his own lips—falls away. The innocent person would no longer have to hack his way through the jungle of uncertainties and technicalities which made all these legal safeguards necessary. He would be able to establish his innocence more easily and directly through science. Indeed, if the reliability of narco-analysis is demonstrated, but it is not received as evidence, an innocent man ready to submit to the testing may be deemed to be deprived unfairly of the right to clear himself.

We can, of course, assume that none would be directly compelled to submit to narcoanalysis, and that such a procedure would be allowed only with the consent of the subject. Not that it would make much practical difference, if a person's consent is required, whether he agrees or refuses to submit to narcoanalysis. Refusal to submit to narcoanalysis would be interpreted, practically if not legally, by the trier of the facts as an admission of guilt—much as jurors construe a defendant's failure to take the stand in a criminal case in a light adverse to him, despite the strongest judicial instructions to the contrary.

As one moves toward extending the reach of narco-analysis in the courts through logic rather than experience, he may encounter critical conflicts in values. Logicians will hold, for the reasons just advanced, that a person actually charged with crime should not complain, since his innocence as well as his guilt can be established through scientific means. But the question will arise whether a witness not under indictment should be compelled to undergo narcoanalysis if by doing so he may implicate himself in the commission of a crime of which he has hitherto been unsuspected. Logically, there should be no difference; the guilty will pay, the innocent be cleared. It is not unlikely, however, that there would be some gagging on such a premise.

This is because the public intuitively looks to those administering justice not only to elicit truth and enforce law, but to satisfy other social and community values. Such protective rules as the privilege against self-incrimination, the presumption of innocence, and the exclusion from evidence of confidential communications between husband and wife, doctor and patient, lawyer and client, all have evolved to maintain the high value the community has set on the grandeur of the individual. Each of these principles subordinates full disclosure of the facts to some other higher social value.

Still closer to our discussion is the inadmissibility of an involuntary confession, even if true. Just recently the United States Supreme Court held the admission into evidence of the confession of one suffering from insanity as violative of the due process clause of the Fourteenth Amendment, not only because the confession was unreliable, but also because it was improperly obtained from one while weak of will and mind. It is, therefore, frequently the case that where investigatory or trial procedures for the disclosure of facts impinge upon deeply held values sustaining the integrity and the dignity of the individual, those values prevail at the expense of the facts. Ultimately, then, the great issue will be what Professor Helen Silving, in a perceptive article, delineated as that of truth versus dignity, as to which she concluded that "in the administration of justice truth is but a means, whereas dignity is an end."

Each of the techniques associated with narco-analysis involves dredging facts from the unconscious that the person interrogated might be unwilling consciously to reveal. To that extent, each of these techniques entails an invasion of his privacy, as well as his freedom of will. Each abrades the dignity of man; and such indignities can become contagious, if not epidemic. Our traditional and adversary system of litigation, though it may not prove to be the most exact medium for ascertaining truth, embodies the democratic emphasis upon respect for human dignity at every step of the way. If we do not act to anticipate, it remains for us to await—and not without anxiety—the balance finally to be struck between the service of dignity and of truth in the trial process as truth comes more surely within reach as a result of scientific validation of fact-finding through unconscious disclosures. The issue posed is, in the end, no less than an uneasy search for the character of our society of the future. For the balance finally struck between dignity and truth in our courts will be cast in the image of a society which has opted either for efficiency or for freedom.

CHAPTER THREE

THE CRIMINAL TRIAL

THERE ARE FEW fictional plots more recurrent than that of the unjustly accused defendant who is vindicated through the brilliant and heroic efforts of his lawyer. The innocent defendant becomes enmeshed in a net of incriminating circumstance, which draws tighter as the story progresses. At the very end of the book or drama—leaving sufficient time on the wireless media for commercials and credits—counsel slashes through and extricates him. To a highly conditioned public, the vindication of the accused is as inexorable an ingredient as the eventual comeuppance of the bad man in a Western thriller; the only suspense hangs on how it will be accomplished.

The fictional lawyer is not only endowed with a shrewd intelligence, but with strength, agility and good looks that are the envy of round-shouldered scholars who have been trained to win cases by poring over books rather than careening around the city in sports cars and finding dead bodies one step ahead of the plodding police. And the make-believe lawyer renders services that author and audience assume are commonplace, but which strike his real-life counterpart as even more incredible than his much flaunted, highly dramatic master strokes. For the Perry Masons

48

seem to have no concern about the overhead expenses that plague the ordinary lawyer in actual practice. They have unlimited time to devote to their client's cause, without regard to his capacity to pay a fee. They can marshal unlimited investigation facilities, at least equal and usually superior to those of the police and prosecutor; and they are called to the case before the accused has hopelessly damaged his chance for a successful defense during questioning while in police custody or in talking to newspapermen. And at the moment of truth, the trial, the lawyers of fiction display a breathtaking virtuosity of legal, psychological and detective strategy that exposes the guilty, saves the innocent, good-naturedly embarrasses the district attorney and satisfies the audience by reinforcing the myth that the scales of the criminal case are so balanced as to assure the triumph of justice.

However, the defense lawyer in fiction may not, and his envious counterpart in reality will not survive, unaltered, the radical changes that are looming in the structure of the criminal trial and in the character of the prosecutor and defense counsel; the shifting values and emphasis appear to be rapidly widening the gap between the criminal trial as blueprinted and organized today and as it was slugged out a generation or two ago.

Just how events are fast fracturing fact from myth in the case of those accused of crime is suggested in Alan Barth's *The Price of Liberty:*

> . . . liberty is being imperiled today for the sake of order . . . in the name of law enforcement, we are now more and more justifying short cuts by the police which involve serious trespasses on procedural

rules intended to limit governmental authority and to insure fairness in the administration of justice. There seems to be a growing disposition in Congress and in the country at large to wink at—indeed, to encourage—these police trespasses.

If these remarks, coming from a layman, appear to overstate the case, then consider the more somber but no less troublesome conclusion reached by Professor Abraham S. Goldstein of the Yale Law School in an article entitled "The State and the Accused: Balance of Advantage in Criminal Procedure," which appeared in the June 1960 issue of the *Yale Law Journal:*

> . . . the hypothetical "accused" can find little to please him in current developments in the criminal trial process. Those developments reflect entirely too little concern about the inherent inequality of litigating position between the expanding state and even the most resourceful individual, much less the vast majority of resourceless ones. And even more fundamentally, they reflect subtle erosion of the accusatorial system, relieving police and prosecutor in many instances of the pressures necessary to maintain their actions at the optimum level of responsibility.

The increasing tipping of the balance between the state and the accused in favor of the state, as described both by Barth and Goldstein, is a matter for anxiety for all. It extends far beyond the apprehensions voiced by the advocates of a "get tough" policy

—apprehensions that the criminal will invoke the legal technicality which will provide an undeserved escape.

For the good citizen in a just society, the prospect of accusation for violation of the criminal law should be fearful. Chief Justice Warren remarked that "when society acts to deprive one of its members of life, liberty or property it takes its most awesome steps." The criminal law processes can implement judgment with the handcuff, the stationhouse, the jail or the death penalty. Older devices of banishment, torture and mutilation may be gone, but there remain forcible removal from family, home, friends and job, and stay in a penal institution enforced by bars and guards. And while the Constitution forbids bills of attainder which, in other times, extended punishment to the criminal's family, the shame and disabilities following on conviction necessarily taint the family as well as the person of the one convicted of a serious offense. Short perhaps of grave illness, there is no more devastating personal calamity than to be in conflict with the authorities charged with administration of the penal laws.

Most of us find ourselves at the precipice of criminality at least once. Annually more than a million persons stand before our judges for sentencing after conviction. Many times that number each year are spared a like fate because of the inadequate facilities or wise and benign discretion of police or prosecutors in the enforcement of the criminal law. Few are exempt from the coverage of a modern penal code which ranges from abandonment through assault, from gambling through homicide, from intoxication in a public place through kidnaping, from libel through lynching, from rape through breaking the Sabbath, from seduction through suicide.

Those counting themselves innocent of the catalogue of traditional crimes may feel some pangs of guilt when reminded of the all-encompassing variety of criminal sanctions now in force to compel compliance with our tax laws. There is also the proliferation of new criminal laws spawned by regulations unavoidable in a burgeoning economy and changing society. It is plainly right, as Professor Gerhard O. W. Mueller of the New York University Law School said recently, that "if criminal law were strictly enforced, we would lack a sufficient number of unconvicted guards to keep the rest of the population behind bars!" There is hardly any freedom from technical guilt—only from prosecution. We are, most of us, profoundly and constantly individually concerned about that terrible engine of power, the processes of the criminal law.

Our universal concern about the criminal law processes is expressed by the state of tension between the monopoly of power we grant to the police and prosecuting authorities to achieve the purposes which underlie the criminal codes and the panoply of rights we accord the accused to protect him against the calloused or corrupt abuse of such power. The great and delicate balance sought is law enforcement which is on the one hand vigorous, yet compassionate and civilized.

Our Constitution came marvelously close to stating the terms necessary to achieve such a balance. It aligned against the power of the federal government such familiar provisions as freedom from unreasonable searches and seizures, the institution of serious criminal charges except where made by a grand jury, double jeopardy, self-incrimination, excessive bail or cruel and inhuman punishments, and the right to a speedy and public trial by jury and the assistance of counsel. And it is constitutionally vouchsafed that the great freedom writ, habeas corpus, will not be suspended except "when in Cases of Rebellion or Invasion the public Safety may require it" and that no person should be convicted for an act which was not a crime when performed (labeled professionally as ex post facto laws).

Most of these safeguards apply to the states as well as to the federal government because of the provisions of the United States Constitution and various state constitutions, rulings of the United States Supreme Court and state statutes and decisions. From these many protective mechanisms there have evolved the great Anglo-American criminal law principles: the presumption of innocence, the burden of the prosecution to prove the guilt of the accused beyond a reasonable doubt, the exclusionary rules of evidence, notably the prohibition of hearsay, and other protective measures forming a set of ground rules to make the constitutional pronouncements meaningful and effective.

The entire structure of our criminal law procedure has, then, been wrought meticulously to protect the individual when he is caught up in that engagement with society which we call a criminal prosecution. Due process—which is legal shorthand for giving an accused a fair deal or "square shake"—jury trial, right to counsel, presumption of innocence, burden of proof and exclusionary rules of evidence are supplied by constitution, statute and common law. In total they are an attempt to assure that loss of life or liberty, or the stigma of conviction, can be sustained only for wrongdoing, not because of the whim or vengeance of an omnipotent sovereign. Each of these restraints contemplates that police and prosecution must act with the decency and civility expected of officialdom in a humane and civilized society, as well as the avoidance of the possibility of the unjust conviction of an innocent man. And yet the totality of the restraints must not be such as to frustrate the legitimate interest of society in the prevention and punishment of behavior harmful to the significant values of a community. The stated ideal in a free yet ordered society is a close, if not reciprocating, balance between power and restraints in the administration of the criminal law.

As we shall see, this idealized balance is being tilted in favor of the state and against the accused as surely as if the blindfolded image of justice had placed her sword onto one of the previously evenly leveled scales. Such an imbalance disturbs beliefs far more profound than a desire for symmetry in the law, or the "sporting" theory of justice which would equalize state and accused as a handicapper would equalize competing race horses to insure a good contest. No system of criminal jurisprudence can eliminate the specter of the conviction of the wrong man. But a certain corollary of the preponderance of power over restraints is an increase in the risk of unjust convictions.

The danger, however, is not confined to the relatively rare jailing or execution of an innocent. Guilt is frequently a matter of degree, and may depend upon the full factual context of the incriminating circumstances. For those accused and guilty of crime, particularly first offenders, the imbalance of power means the inability to require, and the ability only to implore police or prosecutor to show good sense in deciding whether to press charges or what the nature of the charge should be. And for all of us the incalculable risk of a pronounced tilt of the criminal law balance is that it places temptingly ready at hand the tools which have historically served ambition, corruption, overzealous and over-righteous dedication to duty, callousness and contempt for the dignity of others. It is, therefore, a matter of the first importance to see where the balance now stands and what are its prospects.

The principal weights on the accused's scale developed long before the rise of the modern police force and prosecutor. The major elements comprising due process of law derive from the use of the jury system (which brought in its wake, by the eighteenth century, proof by sworn testimony, the right to confrontation and cross-examination, the exclusion of hearsay and the right to counsel) and the struggle from the sixteenth through eighteenth centuries in England and the colonies to curb the excesses in the use of the royal prerogative (which resulted in the privilege against self-incrimination and the guarantee against unreasonable searches and seizures). The procedural rights of the individual molded in these historical matrices are, beyond question, indispensable to our future as they were to our past freedom. Mr. Justice Felix Frankfurter has commented perceptively that the "history of liberty has largely been the history of the observance of procedural safeguards." The troublesome problem, however, is whether the devices conceived to meet the needs of other times are sufficient at present without modernization.

Of course, not all the protections we afford the accused find their origin in events antedating the Constitution and the Bill of Rights. The sum of the features of the criminal procedures prescribed by those documents is an accusatorial system, in which the accuser must state and prove his charges—not the accused his innocence. This implicit characteristic of our constitutional system of criminal law was made explicit during the nineteenth century by the development of the rules of the presumption of innocence and the requirement that the guilt of the accused be proven beyond a reasonable doubt.

The other dominant theme in our constitutional scheme, in addition to the establishment of an accusatorial system, is the right to the due process of law. As due process means a modicum of fairness to the accused and of decency by the state, the concept cannot be and has not been static or frozen in history. Thus, due process and equal protection of the law came relatively recently to require an impartial jury, not one assembled through racial or other forms of obnoxious discrimination. The exclusion from evidence of confessions obtained by force or threats or under inherently coercive circumstances also represents essentially a more recent understanding of the meaning of due process and the privilege against self-incrimination. Again, only during the last forty years have the due process of law and the right to counsel come to include the right to the assignment of counsel to the indigent in all federal prosecutions and in the prosecution of capital offenses in state cases. And less than two years ago the United States Supreme Court held that in state, as well as in federal prosecutions, evidence obtained as a result of an illegal search and seizure may not constitutionally be allowed in evidence.

It remains, however, that most of the accused's rights in the balance between state and accused are of pre-nineteenth-century origin, or at least the finest modern flowering of such rights traces its roots to that time. Unless accorded a most liberal and elastic interpretation, the constitutional statement of those rights as a functioning affirmation is hard pressed by the run of events since then. No matter how far-seeing that statement, it could not and did not anticipate the swelling colossus of police and prosecution facilities, personnel and power which subsequently developed.

Even the concept of the scope of the state's authority and responsibility to apprehend and punish malfeasors, which we accept as deep-grained and fundamental in our society, is relatively modern. Primitive law usually left matters of vengeance or satisfaction to the injured party or his kin. The state's interest in the punishment of wrongdoers gained its principal momentum in England during the twelfth century, when Henry II creatively and ingeniously extended the notion of the "king's peace" to bring within the crown's province all manner of wrongs as breaches of that peace. This process continued until, in the words of Maitland, England's foremost legal historian, the king's peace became "an all-embracing atmosphere." But it was not until late in the nineteenth century, as a result of the state's expansive intervention into every facet of social and economic life, that the present area of criminal jurisdiction was staked out.

The London Metropolitan Police Force, which served as the model for the police departments for our large cities, was organized by Robert (hence "Bobbies") Peel in 1828. Before that time local police forces were far more modest institutions than our modern police departments. American state police forces were not truly started until 1905, and then spread so quickly that by World War II every state had such a corps. And since in our system criminal law enforcement is intended to be principally local, the numerous units exerting federal police authority, and particularly the renowned FBI, did not attain significant proportions until the national government undertook during the last fifty years the social service and regulatory functions which are now part of our established country-wide pattern.

The growth of the modern American police force and prosecutor has been understandably mercurial. From the local constabulary to the national FBI, there are approximately 40,000 police jurisdictions in the United States. The total police personnel in this country numbers about 300,000, including the 25,000 members of the Police Department of the City of New York. Some indication of the additional complement of national, state, city and county prosecutors may be gleaned from the fact that there are eighty-five assistant district attorneys on the staff of the New York County District Attorney's office, earning salaries from $5,500 to $21,500 per annum.

It is, of course, not only with numbers of investigators and prosecutors that the lonely individual is confronted when caught up in the criminal law processes. State, federal and many local police officers and prosecutors are full-time, extensively trained and highly qualified professionals, assisted by the speed and mobility of car and plane, the facility of electrical and electronic communication, the sciences of *moulage*, dactyloscopy, microscopy, ballistics, handwriting analysis and serology, as well as the less acceptable—although regarded as essential by the police— auxiliaries of informer, wire tap, lie detector and narcoanalysis. (It has been estimated that 95 percent of all federal narcotics prosecutions result from the data supplied by informers.) The New York City Police Department Laboratory, manned by about fifty specialists, invokes the learning of the physicist, chemist, biologist, engineer, technician and photographer. And while American criminal law enforcement was properly characterized by the late Bruce Smith, a leading writer on police matters, as "the most complete decentralization of police authority known to the civilized world," the interaction and cooperation of police agencies mean that much of the information and skills of one is available to others. The FBI performs frequent and useful service as a central clearinghouse for the reporting of crime, criminal identification records and the multifarious interstate networks of police teletype and radio.

The dimensions of the accused's adversary become more overwhelming when the state is seen in action. Police, by hypothesis, are society's delegates of force. To prevent or punish crime, police are vested with the symbols and tools of physical power, which is the ultimate authority. Only for the police investigator, then, are detention and search of person and home in aid of inquiry legally permissible. There are, of course, limits prescribed by law to the use of force, arrest and searches by police. But no matter how rigidly the fruits of official transgressions may be excluded from evidence, still those limits rarely find expression in the punishment of the policeman-transgressor.

It is not possible to exaggerate the cumulative physical and psychological impact, in the contest between state and accused, resulting from arrest and interrogation by the police. For all but a few knowledgeable and self-assertive subjects of inquiry, no one of the constitutional safeguards, and not all of them together, can equalize or neutralize the initial advantage which follows from taking the accused into custody and subjecting him at a stationhouse to close questioning by skillful and experienced interrogators, vested with formidable authority and energized by sense of duty or ambition. The interrogation is more than just a series of questions and answers. Professor Goldstein points out that "the accused's fingerprints and footprints may be taken; his blood and urine may be removed, provided the job is done scientifically; his handwriting and voice may be used to involve him in most jurisdictions; he may be required to exhibit himself, in a line-up or otherwise, wearing particular kinds of clothing . . ."

The modern American prosecutor brings to the side of the law enforcement processes powers and capacities no less impressive than those of the police. The late Justice Martin M. Frank, in his *Diary of a District Attorney*, plausibly contended that "the local District Attorney in the smallest or most sparsely populated county wields more power, in some respects, than the governor of the state." The same author described the pre-prosecution capacities of the district attorney as follows:

> . . . the District Attorney in his sole discretion and judgment may initiate criminal proceedings or refrain from doing so. He can order the arrest of anyone suspected of violating the penal law. By exercising the subpoena power of the grand jury, his right to investigate is virtually unlimited, for not only may he seize and examine books and records, but command the appearance of any person, whether public officer or private citizen, who is a resident or physically present anywhere in the state. It is his prerogative to grant complete immunity from prosecution to any person he so chooses to exempt, regardless of the crime that individual has committed. By mutual statutory provisions with some other states, subpoenas issued to residents thereof must be obeyed. With the filing of an indictment, a District Attorney can demand the extradition of a named defendant from any state in the Union and from most foreign countries.

The district attorney's powers begin rather than end with the functions just quoted. Where prosecution is commenced by information rather than indictment by a grand jury, as may be done in many states, the prosecutor is the charging party. In those jurisdictions which require grand jury indictments for the institution of serious charges, it is the district attorney who presents to the grand jury the evidence upon which indictments are based. The degree of the charge laid against an accused—e.g., murder or manslaughter in the case of homicide, larceny or robbery, burglary or unlawful entry—generally lies, in actual practice, within the district attorney's discretion. And the district attorney decides whether the prosecution will recommend a dismissal of the charge or the discharge of the defendant without trial. The district attorney is similarly empowered to recommend to the judge the acceptance of a plea of guilty to the charge or to a lesser charge, and his recommendation is almost invariably followed; and it is for the prosecutor to say what penalty the state will recommend or urge upon sentence.

The present powerful posture of the prosecutor is the result of a transformation which is taking place before our very eyes and which does not entail the uprooting of deep traditions or practices. Under the English common law which the colonists first established on this continent, prosecutions were generally pressed privately through the attorney-general in the name of the king. Not until 1879 did Parliament create the office of director of public prosecutions to supplement the offices of the solicitor-general, the attorney-general and the Treasury Department, the only agencies that previously could be regarded as falling within the category of public prosecutors and which combinedly handled only a small portion of the total number of prosecutions. Justice Frank reports that only 5 percent of prosecutions were conducted by the director of public prosecutions.

Connecticut, in 1704, was the first colony to set up a semblance of our present-day district attorney—public prosecutors engaged in no business other than that of prosecution. The enabling statute read: "Henceforth there shall be in every countie a sober, discreet and religious person appointed by the Countie Courts, to be attorney for the Queen to prosecute and implead in the law all criminals, and to do all other things necessary or convenient as an attorney to suppress vice and immoralities." With the turn of the nineteenth century the office of public prosecutor had become an integral part of the administration of American justice.

Every indication presages no abatement of the growth of power of our law enforcement agencies in the foreseeable future. Crime, not a lust for power, is the cause for that growth. The staggering crime statistics leave no doubt of the future expansion of the roles of police and prosecutors: 2,000,000 major crimes reported per year, including theft, rape, robbery, murder and assault; in New York City on an average day $150,000 in property is stolen, one person murdered, three rapes reported, 103 homes burglarized, and 33 assaults and 131 grand larcenies committed. Alan Barth quotes J. Edgar Hoover as saying in 1960:

> Today we find ourselves confronted with the worst era of lawlessness in the Nation's history. Each twenty seconds another serious crime is added to the Nation's total. A murder, forcible rape or assault to kill is committed every four minutes. There is a burglary every forty-six seconds; a robbery every seven minutes; and thirty-three automobiles are stolen every hour.

Still more appalling is the enormity of organized and syndicated crime dealing in gambling, vice, narcotics and illegal liquor. Traditional crimes take

$500,000,000 of our sustenance annually. Organized crime, stemming from Prohibition days, grosses $7,500,000,000 and gambling $20,000,000,000. With stakes so high it is no surprise to hear from a former United States attorney for the Southern District of New York, Paul Williams, that crime "has become better organized and criminals often operate with the best legal and accounting advice. They have adopted corporate methods in the handling of vast enterprises." Confronted by such a deeply embedded parasite in the body of society, which debilitates by corruption of politics and morals as well as devours victims' money, we are bound to reinforce the men and facilities who act as antibodies. In the process of thus enlarging the forces necessary to cope with crime we shall, however, inevitably overmatch the already limited resources of the individual who is accused but innocent of crime; or who, though guilty, is subjected to a charge or penalty not sanctioned by ordinary decency or good judgment.

Pitted against the crushing complex of the power of police and prosecutor, the accused individual is helpless except for the countervailing defenses erected by the Constitution, and even with those he may be pitifully frail.

For the accused individual the Constitution barely moves from paper to reality without the help of counsel. It may be, as Chief Justice Charles Evans Hughes observed, that the Constitution is what the judges say it is; but for the accused the Constitution is what his lawyer makes of it. Withhold counsel as paladin of the Constitution, and the average accused enjoys only the aura but not the substance of constitutional right. Yet a recent report by a special committee of the Association of the Bar of the City of New York and the National Legal Aid Association, entitled *Equal Justice for the Accused,* estimates "that approximately 60 per cent of those charged with crime cannot afford to employ counsel" and that "in many jurisdictions, this need for representation is not being met by any system."

Nine states, and particularly California and Illinois, provide some of their impecunious defendants with public defender systems. Legal Aid and Voluntary Defender societies exist in Boston, Philadelphia, New York City and Washington, D.C., and Congress has considered the establishment of a public defender system for the federal courts. New York City, under a permissive statute enacted in 1961, appropriated $100,000 toward the annual operating expenses of the Legal Aid Society. But today, and for some time to come, many accused of crime must face a well-armed adversary without the benefit of counsel carrying even the most rudimentary spear.

The United States Supreme Court has shown a sensitive solicitude about the accused's right to counsel, and particularly concerning the rights of the indigent accused. In 1956, in holding that a state prisoner could not be denied an appeal because of his inability to buy the minutes of his trial, the Court said: "There can be no equal justice where the kind of trial a man gets depends on the amount of money he has." But by the time a criminal case reaches the appeal stage, a good deal of irreparable damage may have been done. For even those who can afford counsel, and certainly those who cannot pay for a lawyer, are typically without the presence or advice of counsel during the critical investigative phase of law enforcement. Arrest and questioning need not be announced in advance. Once in custody there is not usually recourse to counsel before interrogation begins. Contrary to popular belief, police are not obliged to advise an accused under interrogation of the right to counsel or to provide counsel for him if he is indigent.

It is, of course, understandable that even enlightened police investigators, acting honorably by contemporary standards, do not encourage or facilitate contact between suspect and lawyer. Such communication might silence someone otherwise inclined to be "cooperative." The Constitution does not expressly, or by judicial construction, require the police questioning a suspect to warn of the risk of self-incrimination or to explain the right to keep silent. By contrast, English police practices, codified as the Judges' Rules, require that "whenever a police officer has made up his mind to charge a person with crime, he should first caution such person before asking any questions . . . 'Do you wish to say anything in answer to the charge? You are not obliged to say anything unless you wish to do so, but whatever you say will be taken down in writing and may be given in evidence.'" While it is invariably required by statute in this country that a person under arrest must be brought promptly by the police before a judicial hearing officer to determine the propriety of the detention and to fix bail, the United States Supreme Court has many times sustained state court convictions based upon confessions obtained during prolonged detention before the holding of the specified hearing. Only in federal prosecutions does the failure promptly to arraign an accused furnish automatic grounds for the judicial rejection of any incriminating statement taken during the improper detention. Yet, as the late Senator Hennings noted, "The seeds of coercion sprout readily in the soil of illegal detention."

As matters now stand, investigators cannot be expected, and are usually not required to suggest or facilitate the presence of counsel. Yet the absence of counsel during detention and interrogation by the police, when the accused does not enjoy the security of family or friends, or the watchful and protective presence of court, jury or public, may be fatal to any subsequent defense. The effect of the usual absence of counsel while the suspect is under police arrest and examination is to convert our criminal law *pro tanto* from an accusatorial to an inquisitorial system. Advice and benefit of counsel after such interrogation has been exhausted is still valuable, but too often anticlimactic; so, too, is the package of constitutional safeguards looking to preserve an accusatorial process which contemplates the proof of guilt by the accuser without the assistance of the accused.

The inability to raise bail is another pretrial factor that often diminishes or defeats a defendant's opportunity to prepare his defense appropriately. Our juridical and constitutional concept of the function of bail is perhaps the most enlightened in the entire world. Presumably we do not withhold or fix unreasonable bail out of apprehension that the defendant will engage in crime while awaiting trial or that he will tamper with the prosecution's evidence or seek to influence its witnesses. In our system bail is based upon the risk that the defendant will not appear for court action. This, in turn, depends upon the defendant's devotion to his family, his church, union and other roots in the community, the gravity of the charge, his record and his financial status and employment background. Yet, in practice, bail experience is still another manifestation of the shifting balance between state and accused.

Very often defendants who are unable to furnish bail and are later found innocent are lodged in temporary detention institutions which represent harsher and more oppressive punishment than the jail sentences or suspended sentences which may be meted out to other defendants after conviction. In most cases, having these considerations in mind, judges earnestly try to fix bail in amounts they do not regard as excessive. The exceptions are usually well publicized, as when judges accede to the district attorney's exhortation to set inordinately high bail for notorious defendants, or when a broad drive is on against certain categories of defendants, such as gamblers, narcotic users or sellers, etc.

Yet, even when bail is fixed at what most people would regard as low or moderate limits, a surprisingly large number of defendants are unable to raise it. Such a defendant, in jail during the period he is presumably preparing his defense, is obviously placed at a serious disadvantage in his contest with the prosecuting authorities. Supreme Court Justice Douglas mentioned, in an opinion in 1960, that " . . . in the case of an indigent defendant, the fixing of bail in even a modest amount may have the practical effect of denying him release. The wrong done by denying release is not limited to the denial of freedom alone. That denial may have other consequences. In case of reversal, he will have served all or part of a sentence under an erroneous judgment . . ." A 1958 study of the administration of bail in New York City by the University of Pennsylvania Law School confirms Justice Douglas' views. It revealed that in 28 percent of the cases defendants were unable to furnish as little as $500 bail; 38 percent were unable to raise $1,000; 45 percent could not furnish $2,000; and 63 percent could not raise bail in the amount of $2,500. The fact that only 3 percent of all defendants covered by the report were released on their own recognizance by magistrates—that is, released without depositing cash or bond in any amount—points up the need for serious study and experimentation in the elimination of bail altogether in the generality of cases, with exceptions made when doubt is raised as to whether a defendant will appear without bail.

Of course, in any such experiment ample auxiliary services should be afforded the courts, so that prompt investigations and reports, when necessary, could be made for the guidance of the judge. We predict the courts would not be deluged with resultant flights from the jurisdiction. And aside from the cost in human dignity, enormous savings could be effected in the cost of maintaining jails for the temporary detention of defendants awaiting trial and grand jury action.

At the trial stage the growing imbalance between state and accused is another reminder that constitutional rights are not self-enforcing and, unless implemented, are inadequate to dissipate the twentieth-century disparity between the resources available to the criminal trial combatants. In those criminal cases which go through trial, convictions are returned at the rate of about seven out of ten. When convictions after trial are added to convictions after guilty pleas, the rate of convictions reaches the level of 90 percent of all prosecutions in most jurisdictions and may be as high as 98 percent in others. Our criminal trial processes are, therefore, hardly the technicality-mined booby traps for prosecutors imagined by laymen. There can be no way of verifying the correlation between actual guilt and convictions or between actual innocence and acquittals. But we do know, because of the documentation by the late Professor Edwin M. Borchard in his *Convicting the Innocent* and by the late United States Circuit Court of Appeals Judge Jerome Frank and his daughter Barbara in their book *Not Guilty*, that enough instances of conviction of innocents exist to challenge the conscience of the community.

In discussing the trial of a criminal charge we may, at the outset, put to one side the accused's constitutional privilege to sit silent through the trial and rely solely upon the inability of the prosecution to prove its case. A recent analysis of data from the Administrative Office of the United States Courts showed that in 99 percent of all criminal cases tried in the federal courts defendants who did not testify on their own behalf were convicted by juries. The accused has little choice other than to attempt to prove his innocence. While the prosecutor may not comment upon the defendant's failure to take the stand, there is always at least one court-wise juror who will advise his colleagues authoritatively that the reason for the defendant's refusal to testify is that he must have a long record of convictions.

Under the rules of evidence, even if a defendant has had a dozen previous convictions, no proof of this record can be introduced unless he testifies. This rule of evidence was designed to protect the defendant, so that a jury would not draw the inference that because he had committed other crimes he probably perpetrated the one for which he is standing trial, or that a jury may not be tempted to say he is a bad lot anyway and the community is better off by removing him from its midst. But if the defendant does testify, his credibility is placed in issue, like that of any other witness, and it may be assailed by showing past illegal or immoral acts—whether they resulted in conviction of crimes or not—that would indicate he is not likely to be an apostle of truth on the witness stand. Aware of jury sophistication, wise lawyers often feel constrained to put defendants with spotless records on the stand, although the weakness of the prosecution's case would ordinarily dictate that exposure of the defendant to cross-examination is a wholly unnecessary risk.

During trial the accused is opposed by a prosecutor who is obliged by oath and impelled by persuasion or ambition or vanity or adversary ardor to use all the skill and resources at his disposal to convict. When a criminal case reaches the point of trial the prosecutor is then the advocate for the community seeking to bring the criminal to justice, with all the psychological spur and stimulus of an attorney in an adversary proceeding. Whitney North Seymour, Jr., described the prosecutor at a trial as a "full-fledged fighting advocate; and he should be. He must act with candor and fairness, but he must also fight for his cause. To do otherwise would be to violate his duty in the most real sense." In support of this effort, the prosecutor, thus postured and stimulated, has all the investigative facilities and materials we have mentioned as well as the prestige of his office and the sharp edge of his expertise.

The accused alone is, of course, seldom if ever a match for the prosecutor at a trial. Trial of a case, especially a criminal case, is an art for which few lawyers and no laymen are suited. Only through the intervention of trial counsel can the trial procedures and evidentiary rules intended to safeguard the accused on trial be effectively invoked. Professor David Fellman has been quoted as saying that the defendant in a criminal case "needs a lawyer as urgently as a sick man needs a doctor, and in many instances even more urgently, for while nature often heals the sick without outside aid, it seems to have little concern for the plight of the accused." Without counsel there can be no full defense; and it bears repetition that "60 percent of those charged with crime cannot afford to employ counsel."

There are no statistics to tell us how many, in addition to the indigent 60 percent, cannot afford to employ counsel as competent as the prosecutor. Newman Levy, a long-time New York criminal trial lawyer, has observed that "many lawyers" are restrained from taking on criminal cases "by the absurd belief that criminal practice is *déclassé*." At least an equally cogent reason is the mundane one that the practice of criminal law often yields too little money for too much work. Most persons on trial for crimes are not affluent, and the criminal law bar can complain ruefully that crime does not pay—for anyone.

Few can finance the time and expense necessary for able counsel to study the charges and the applicable law, interview the accused and the witnesses thoroughly, investigate all the surrounding circumstances, appear and plead upon arraignment, arrange for bail, make the necessary pretrial motions which will probe the legal weaknesses of the prosecution or elicit the factual data in the possession of the prosecution, engage in conferences and negotiations with the prosecutor's office looking toward some mutually satisfactory disposition, and then, if trial eventuates, marshal and prepare the proof and the law to be presented on behalf of the defendant, wait to be reached for trial, pick a jury and then go forth to the intensely arduous job of trial itself. It is no reflection on the many fine and competent lawyers engaged in criminal law practice to say that in only relatively few of all criminal cases has the accused enjoyed as full and effective benefit of counsel as the accuser receives from offices so rich in resources as those of the United States attorney or the district attorney.

Judge Jerome Frank in an opinion correctly appraised the importance of investigation preparatory to trial:

> . . . The best lawyer in the world cannot competently defend an accused person if the lawyer cannot obtain existing evidence crucial to the defense, e.g., if the defendant cannot pay the fee of an investigator to find a pivotal missing witness or a necessary document, or that of an expert accountant or mining engineer or chemist.

There are, at present, only meager means of gaining for a defendant the desirable investigative facilities except by way of the defendant's purse, and few are long or full enough to meet the bill. It is instructive to learn from the same opinion of Judge Frank that it has, for more than seventy years, been the practice in Scandinavia

> . . . to place the police department and the office of the prosecutor equally at the service of the defense and the prosecution; defense counsel may have these agencies, at government expense, make all necessary investigations, including searches for witnesses and documents and analyses by handwriting, medical or chemical experts; and the prosecution is responsible for producing at trial the witnesses called by the accused as well as all other evidence he wishes introduced—again at government expense.

This is the kind of collaboration that truly presents the prosecutor as the protector of the innocent as well as the foe of the guilty. In most countries, including the United States, it is not fully obtainable; and most prosecutors shield their resources and evidence from the defense, as lawyers do in adversary proceedings. Many generations of conditioning in the adversary tradition cannot be reformed into new attitudes by the best-intentioned of directives or the promulgation of the fairest ground rules. The hope for the future, or at least the discernible future in this country, would seem to lie not in an accused having a call upon or sharing official resources, but in matching them through the unique, fast-growing and invaluable national network of public defenders and legal aid groups that are either privately supported or sustained by both governmental and private funds. Most of these organizations, with dedicated personnel, perform miracles on a tiny fraction of the funds and facilities afforded police and prosecutors.

Government should move toward equalizing the capacities of the contending agencies by appropriating for defense sums approximating the enormous amounts budgeted for investigation and prosecution. The current concept of legal defense would be uplifted if counsel for the indigent were paid decent salaries and afforded tenure and the same measure of assistance and auxiliary services now available to their adversaries. The innovation could hasten the acceptance of the Scandinavian ideal and the translation of the prosecution's adversary attitude into a more collaborative one, after the extravagance and inefficiency of maintaining two organizations to investigate the same cases had become apparent. And under such favorable auspices, defense attorneys of the Clarence Darrow caliber could again emerge to match the color and popularity of prosecutors like William P. Borah and William Travers Jerome.

In the high percentage of all criminal cases which result in conviction, the case is concluded by the imposition of sentence. This function is performed by the trial judge. Apart from those instances where the verdict by law dictates the exact sentence, the punishment to be meted out is left to the discretion of the trial judge within the usually wide range of limits fixed by the statute. In 1949 the United States Supreme Court settled the proposition that, in the exercise of this discretion, the judge may act upon the basis of information and reports concerning the defendant's character and habits—reports never disclosed to the defendant, never tested by confrontation and cross-examination in a courtroom, and inadmissible as formal evidence. We discuss elsewhere the reasons which impelled a procedure deviating so far from the norms which we usually associate with the trial and disposition of a criminal charge, and for pragmatic reasons recognize that it cannot be condemned out of hand. At this juncture the point of emphasis is that upon sentence, once again, the state stands at a palpable advantage vis-à-vis the accused.

It may be said that many of the existing and evolving erosions of the accused's position have meant a correlative improvement in the state's ability to apprehend and punish wrongdoers. But more convictions, even of the guilty, are not necessarily a sufficient justification for less protection to the accused. The instinct which underlies the balance between state and accused proposed by our Constitution is not just to attain efficiency in law enforcement. It was surely understood, for example, long before the advent of the well-cushioned racketeer and organized crime, that the adoption of the privilege against self-incrimination and the prohibition against unauthorized searches and seizures would impede the state in the investigation of crime, to the advantage of guilty as well as innocent suspects. It was profoundly believed, however, that the hazard of unsolved and unpunished crime was preferable to an excess of power in the hands of the state. Accordingly, the choice made at the birth of the nation was to risk unpunished crime rather than to risk the state's abuse of power. It is this choice which is memorialized in the Constitution and the Bill of Rights, and it is this choice which is and will be increasingly challenged by current and future developments in our criminal law enforcement processes.

Whatever the individual features of each of the developments that are woven into the present-day pattern of prosecution, in sum they reflect the shifting balance between state and accused. It is this full pattern which needs articulation and then reasoned anticipation. It is unwise, as it is unfair to our respected and cherished values, to allow a matter so integral to a free society as the balance between state and accused to be realigned piecemeal and without some knowledgeable choice among the fragments made possible by periodic scrutiny of the entire evolving canvas. Neither public nor profession can continue to rest comfortably with old shibboleths about the constitutional rights of an accused—regularly reinforced by the mass media folklore on the subject—while reality drastically redefines those rights. In this area of the judicial process, as in the others reviewed, the need is to confront emerging forces before they assume proportions which leave no room for choice. In matters which count, the ripple of the present cannot be permitted to become the tidal wave of the future.

CHAPTER FOUR

THE COURT

AT THE HEART of the litigation process is the presentation of proof by opposing lawyers in which *only* the evidence submitted in court—under oath and subject to confrontation and cross-examination—may be taken into account in reaching a decision. The trial process is the sophisticated mode of deciding conflict peaceably in a courtroom, rather than through force. Trained professionals conduct rational inquiry into the disputed facts and, applying wise, well-grooved rules, arrive at judgment. The trial process is the formula prescribed by Anglo-Saxon tradition for settling unresolved quarrels that really matter.

Today, however, the vaunted trial process, the embodiment of the due process we proclaim as the foundation of American justice, is losing ground steadily as a means of testing out opposing claims. Great chunks of controversy now come before nonjudicial tribunals, and many of those quarrels which remain in the courts are being tried in ways which would have been rejected as shocking by judicial traditionalists of another time.

All manner of commercial and labor disputes, even certain aspects of matrimonial differences, are now brought to arbitration, where rules of evidence do not apply and lawyers frequently play no part, either as presiding officers or advocates. Conflicts with government are generally decided by administrative agencies which are not bound to use lawyers or the rules of evidence followed in court. Besides enforcing controls in numerous areas of agriculture, industry, transportation and finance, administrators now have the power of vital decision over jobs, loyalty status, deportability and even citizenship in their responsibility for the conduct of almost ten million government-paid personnel, loyalty-security programs and nationality and immigration laws. Millions of claims which flow from personal injuries sustained while at work are now handled by workmen's compensation commissions or boards. Private tribunals settling pension, intra-union, and intra-industry disputes also bypass courts, judges, lawyers and rules of evidence. There has been, in short, a flight from the courts in many areas of litigation—and in each instance there has been much preliminary beating of wings against the delays and technicalities of the courts. A closer look at the causes and consequences of the exodus explains why we can expect a good deal more of this for the future.

Arbitration follows where parties agree to have some present or future dispute heard and decided by private nonjudicial machinery without rules of evidence and often without benefit of lawyers. The procedure is not new. Merchants have been submitting their arguments to other merchants for decision since at least the thirteenth century in England. Mercantile courts and juries, as well as merchant arbitrators, were part of the English system of handling commercial disputes. Arbitration was well known to enterprising businessmen in the colonies, the arbitration of disputes being one of the purposes for founding the New York Chamber of Commerce in 1768. It is a procedure that has endeared itself to impatient businessmen and others who believe, sometimes mistakenly, that it is the method of securing swift, efficient and inexpensive justice.

For a time arbitration encountered judicial hostility as nineteenth-century courts sought jealously to prevent incursions by private tribunals into areas previously occupied exclusively by the judiciary. In a futile attempt to staunch the seepage from courts to arbitration, judges declared that parties to a controversy could not, by private agreement, oust courts of jurisdiction. By 1925, however, the Federal Arbitration Act was adopted, following by five years the pioneering New York Arbitration Act. Now arbitration agreements are respected and an arbitration award based upon a valid contract is considered final, binding and enforceable in our state and federal courts unless tainted by fraud, corruption or serious procedural irregularity.

The volume of disputes which are arbitrated instead of litigated in the courts is enormous. Most court litigation concerns money and too often represents a poor investment for the businessman who finds that the cost in time and lawyers' fees often converts a legal victory into a financial loss. With rare exceptions the party prevailing in a lawsuit in this country will recover only nominal costs which do not begin to defray his actual expenditures. For example, he may pay a legal fee of ten thousand dollars and be awarded one or two hundred dollars in costs. In England, by comparison, the costs payable to the successful party will include his reasonable counsel fees among the other expenses of litigation.

The practical man does not hesitate to pass up a highly developed system offering him expensive and slow-moving procedural safeguards in favor of the informality of arbitration, especially when his mind's eye drifts from a batch of lawyers discoursing in legal jargon in a somber courtroom to a small group of his fellow businessmen who speak his language in a cozy office. As a result, arbitration is used not only when parties agree to arbitrate an existing dispute, but also when they agree at the outset of their relationship that any future controversy between them will be arbitrated. Both kinds of arbitration agreement are judicially enforceable. A party to an agreement to arbitrate cannot later change his mind and bring the argument to court for adjudication; upon timely objection, he will be told that the matter must be arbitrated, not litigated.

Agreements to arbitrate future disputes find their way into every kind of contractual arrangement. An increasing number of labor contracts commit unresolved grievances and job security and disciplinary matters to arbitration; and it is not uncommon for subjects of collective bargaining, such as wages, hours, vacations and other working conditions, to be assigned to arbitration after negotiation has been exhausted. A series of recent United States Supreme Court decisions has accorded particular vitality to labor contracts seeking to replace strikes and injunctions with arbitration.

In commerce, where it originated, arbitration is used even more widely. Individual arbitration agreements are boilerplate in sales transactions and may be found in printed sales order forms and standard form contracts as well as in contracts of international trade. Trade associations, the American Arbitration Association, the International Chamber of Commerce and local Chambers of Commerce provide established machinery for the arbitration of commercial disputes. A recently published study by Professor Soia Mentschikoff of the University of Chicago Law School indicates that more than 85 percent of the associations queried reported that arbitration was used by their membership. Another highly qualified observer has found that in New York City alone, sixty trade associations have arbitration tribunals to which conflicts involving their members are brought.

Professor Mentschikoff's close study of the work load of the American Arbitration Association led her to the conclusion that the arbitration case load handled by that Association in New York City from 1947 to 1950 "is somewhat greater than the number of cases of a comparable nature filed in the United States District Court for the Southern District of New York"—the latter being the busiest federal court in the country, with jurisdiction over New York, Bronx and Westchester Counties. In the last five years the average volume of cases filed with the Association has increased almost 50 percent over the 1947–50 figures.

That the expanding arbitration process is displacement of the judicial process, and not a duplication, is clear. The officer presiding over a typical judicial trial is a disinterested, full-time, legally trained professional. He presides in a court to which the parties over which it has jurisdiction are compelled to repair for relief. Unlike the arbitration tribunal, courts and judges are constituted and chosen by society in general, not by the parties to the dispute.

Few of the characteristics of the judge mark the arbitrator. He need not be a lawyer; he may be selected by the parties; he can be chosen for his specialized knowledge of the subject matter of the dispute rather than of the law; and he may have been selected just for the single arbitration, being otherwise engaged for his livelihood. The trial process involves sworn testimony, decision based upon competent proof and adherence to precedents in matters of law. Arbitration does not require testimony under oath, a formal record, confinement of proof to rules of evidence or the following of prior decisions. Arbitration allows the difference between the parties to be compromised. Where the law requires an all-or-nothing decision, the arbitrator may simply decide to split the difference in whatever proportions he deems fair. Seldom is such a compromise discernible, as arbitrators rarely need give reasons for their awards. And the right to appeal from mistakes, so valued in Anglo-American law, is virtually non-existent in arbitration.

Much of this reflects the limited roles of lawyers in arbitration. Professor Mentschikoff reports that:

. . . In almost all self-contained trade associations and exchanges . . . lawyer participation in the arbitration proceedings is either forbidden or discouraged, and very few of the arbitrators are lawyers or law-trained. We frequently heard, both orally and in writing, that lawyer participation was not desired for two reasons: (1) lawyers did not understand the business usages and practices that were typically involved in adjudicating the dispute and were therefore not helpful; and (2) lawyers made the proceedings unduly technical and tended to create unnecessary delays. This second complaint about lawyers has some support in our analysis of the Association records. Both delays in the selection of arbitrators and postponements between hearings occur more frequently in cases in which the parties are represented by attorneys. When both parties were represented by attorneys, 43 per cent of the cases were decided in less than 90 days and 21 per cent in less than 60 days. When neither party brought an attorney, 78 per cent of the cases were decided in less than 90 days and 49 per cent in less than 60 days. Of course, the figures also showed that attorneys were more likely to be employed as the amount involved in the case became larger.

Arbitration can be speedy, cheap, expert and unencumbered by the formal and formidable machinery of the courts. Now that it has all the earmarks of institutionalization, it has the momentum of habit and mechanism as well as utility to ensure its continued expansion. Any reversal of the trend is unlikely as businessmen, guided by watch and wallet, turn to the now familiar and practical technique of arbitration. The consequence is that huge sectors of those controverted matters which would otherwise be governed by our elaborate system of due process of law are now committed to the informal and flexible —but nonjudicial—process of arbitration. This is not to decry, but to describe an inexorable development.

The life blood of the courts has likewise flowed

copiously into the administrative agencies that resolve disputes in which government has an interest.
The story of the growth of administrative agencies is
now too well known to bear extensive rehearsal.
What is worth telling, however, is the relatively un-
heralded story of the increasing administrative adjudication of personal rights and freedoms which are
commonly believed to be safeguarded by the guarantees associated with the judicial trial process.

In its report of 1941, the Attorney General's Committee on Administrative Procedure in Government
Agencies remarked that "the administrative process
in the Federal Government is not new. On the contrary, it is as old as the Government itself; and its
growth has been virtually as steady as that of the
Statutes at Large." Yet, as late as 1886, Woodrow
Wilson referred to public administration as "a foreign
science speaking very little of the language of English
or American principle. It employs only foreign
tongues; it utters none but what are to our minds
alien ideas." At the same time, the great English
constitutional jurist, Albert Dicey, in talking of administrative law, said that it was without name in the
English language: "The want of a name arises at
bottom from our non-recognition of the thing itself."
By the end of Franklin D. Roosevelt's first term,
names for the administrative process were no longer
lacking; endless alphabetical combinations and per-
mutations were required to denominate great and
continuing agencies such as the ICC, FTC, FPC,
FCC, FDIC, SEC, NLRB, etc., as well as the innumerable smaller and more transient bureaucracies.

The principal concern of the early federal, state
and local agencies was the regulation of business

practices and the social services assumed by government. Big business inevitably meant busy government to protect against commercial excesses and individual misfortunes. Government could not, of course, begin to enforce its multitudinous mandates except through specialized agencies developed to administer many laws on a day-to-day basis. Almost from the beginning the work of administrative agencies shaded from administration into adjudication—the job usually associated with courts. The Attorney General's Committee mentioned before pointed out that administrative adjudication occurs "where the differences between private interests or between private interests and public officials have not been capable of solution by informal methods but have proved sufficiently irreconcilable to require settlement through formal public proceedings in which the parties have an opportunity to present their own and attack the others' evidence and arguments before an official body with authority to decide the controversy." This definition is, of course, indistinguishable from the essential elements of the judicial process. And it is this identity of function which has provided the storm center of controversy over administrative agencies.

Neither the economic regulation nor the social services performed by administrative agencies endeared the administrative process to those unsympathetic to governmental restraints of business or government spending of tax moneys. For more than a decade, starting in the early 1930s, administrative agencies were to some "the headless fourth branch of government," "the new despotism." Whenever adjudication by administrative agencies departed from traditional trial processes, deviation from due process was loudly claimed. Administrative hearing officers, usually associated with the agency prosecuting the charge and too frequently blended—to the erosion of neutrality—with the agency's prosecuting and investigatory personnel, were contrasted with the detached and disinterested quality of the traditional judge. The broader scope of admissibility of evidence in administrative hearings was compared unfavorably with the careful court rules of materiality, relevancy and competency, and particularly the exclusion of hearsay, all calculated to protect the parties in judicial trials. Liberals, however, mustered comparable hyperbole to defend the dedicated expertise of administrative agencies and the supposed superiority of the administrative process over the archaisms of the judicial process.

No doubt much of the criticism and defense of the administrative adjudicatory process stemmed from what was done, not from how it was done. The real pinch, to the critics, was that government presumed, more than ever before, to govern. But not all their talk was mere rationalization. Those who had seen, first hand, the rise of totalitarianism in Europe, warned that administrative techniques that could be justified for the regulation of property could also be too easily extended to the regulation of liberty. The late Dr. Alexander Pekelis, a brilliant European lawyer and scholar, observed that:

When we European liberals were first faced with the dispute between the American liberals and the American conservatives concerning the questions of administrative law and administrative discretion, the first impulse of many of us was to tell the American liberals of our European experience, to warn them against the inherent dangers of the rise of administrative discretion, and to tell them that we could vouch for the truth of the stand of the American conservatives.

Under politically conservative leadership Congress adopted the Federal Administrative Procedure Act of 1946. That act sets many of the old quarrels to rest. Hearing officers are not to "be responsible to or subject to the supervision or direction of any officer, employee or agent engaged in the investigative or prosecuting functions of any agency. No officer, employee, or agent engaged in the performance of investigative or prosecuting functions for any agency in any case shall, in that or a factually related case, participate or advise in the decision . . ." Decisions are required to be based exclusively upon the testimony and exhibits presented to the hearing officer, and "every agency shall as a matter of policy provide for the exclusion of irrelevant, immaterial, or unduly repetitious evidence and no sanction shall be imposed or rule or order be issued except upon consideration of the whole record or such portions thereof as may be cited by any party and as supported by and in accordance with the reliable, probative, and substantial evidence. Every party shall have the right to present his case or defense by oral or documentary evidence, to submit rebuttal evidence, and to conduct such cross-examination as may be required for a full and true disclosure of the facts."

Just at the point that the conservative critics of administrative agencies gained the ascendancy over the liberal defenders of those agencies, a most extraordinary reversal of attitudes on the part of liberals and conservatives occurred. After World War II administrative agencies became increasingly involved in the enforcement of laws and attitudes reflecting our vigorous reaction to the menace of communism. Loyalty-security programs, immigration and travel restrictions, postal censorship, etc., etc., all brought into play the same administrative process which the liberals had sought to nurture and the conservatives to curtail. As the process came to deal more with the freedom of people as compared with the freedom of property, it acquired both new foes and new friends. Professor Walter Gellhorn of Columbia Law School described what happened in this way:

> During the period in which these and other new powers have been granted or old ones fortified, the former friends and the former detractors of the administrative process have been circumnavigating the globe of government, traveling in opposite directions. The friends, starting from a point on the globe that might be labeled extreme support, have now traveled all the way to the station of extreme fear. The detractors, starting from extreme fear, have seemingly reached the point from which the friends had so recently departed.

The ultimate irony of the switch of roles has been the unsuccessful effort of liberals to have the safeguards of the Administrative Procedure Act—the product of conservative criticism of an earlier day— applied by statute to loyalty hearings or to proceedings involving the exclusion or deportation of immigrants or the denaturalization or denationalization of citizens.

Sheer necessity dictates the continuously increasing allocation of disputes to administrative tribunals. It is now inconceivable that the vast numbers of administrative adjudications could possibly be rechanneled into the courts without reversing a fixed trend and swamping the judicial plant in the process. It is also too late to expect that the nonjudicial features of administrative adjudication will be recast in the judicial image. The administrative process has sufficiently demonstrated its capacity to reach fair judgment without aping the judicial process in each detail. What remains is the issue whether the administrative process, now no longer just a guardian in the economic realm but also a regulator of many personal liberties and freedoms, can incorporate into its adjudicatory function an appropriate analogue to the values of and safeguards for the dignity and integrity of the individual that have been evolved by the judiciary.

Even the court-retained residuum of cases that have resisted the siren call of administrative tribunals must recognize the climate of change. The modern criminal sentencing procedure is typical of current inroads into traditional notions of how courts go about their work. Sentencing is the function of the trial judge and, within the minimum and maximum sentences which may be prescribed by statute, his discretion is virtually absolute and seldom disturbed by an appellate court. In most states, and in the federal jurisdiction, the sentencing judge may request and use presentence reports prepared by probation officers. These reports, calculated to aid the judge in arriving at a wise judgment as to sentence, are the product of out-of-court investigations by persons trained in social work. Neighbors, friends, family and business associates may be questioned out of the presence of the defendant, counsel, judge or jury, and their views presented to the judge in confidential reports. Information is necessarily accumulated pursuant to criteria that are different from the standards of competency and admissibility used in a trial. Frequently, in order to assure full cooperation from sources of information, neither the defendant nor his counsel may see the report; and, with few exceptions, the defendant may not confront or cross-examine either the probation officer or the sources of the report.

This means that the critical issue of whether one convicted of crime is to go to jail and, if so, for how long, is decided by the use of sheer hearsay with which the defendant is not confronted and which he has no opportunity to test by cross-examination or to rebut by evidence. One law review writer has characterized the result of "the new penology" as vesting "in judges and parole and probation agencies the greatest degree of uncontrolled power over the liberty of human beings that one can find in the legal system." In a 1949 case, however, the United States Supreme Court sustained the constitutionality of many of the described features of the sentencing procedures.

In that case the trial judge, acting upon information contained in a presentence report, imposed the death penalty in disregard of a jury recommendation of a life sentence. Mr. Justice Black, the member of the Supreme Court often most solicitous of the rights of an accused to a full and fair judicial trial, wrote the opinion for the Court. He pointed out that long tradition allowed considerable latitude to a judge concerning the kind of evidence and information to be considered on sentencing. In addition, Mr. Justice Black said:

> ... We must recognize that most of the information now relied upon by judges to guide them in the intelligent imposition of sentences would be unavailable if information were restricted to that given in open court by witnesses subject to cross-examination. And the modern probation report draws on information concerning every aspect of a defendant's life. The type and extent of this information make totally impractical if not impossible open court testimony with cross-examination. Such a procedure could endlessly delay criminal administration in a retrial of collateral issues.

Extrajudicial investigation in sentencing uses the social science disciplines and resources to provide the fullest possible insight into the individual whose personality and character are weighed in the sentencing procedure. The inquiry is not, as in the antecedent trial, to reconstruct some past event in order to determine guilt or innocence; the inquiry is that of the social worker into the potential for good or evil, harm or usefulness, in the individual to be sentenced. Such an investigation is extrajudicial because it is not conducted within the framework of contending lawyers and strict rules of evidence. Obviously, however, it is not the sentencing procedure alone that thus wrenches the judicial process loose from its traditional moorings. Wherever an adjudication is to be adapted to the unique character of an individual the pull is away from the courtroom and to the field.

This is particularly notable when the young or the family bring their problems to court.

Few current developments have more radically transformed court procedures than the modern judicial ingestion of the problems of the home. From the eleventh century to Henry VIII, secular courts were concerned only with the property incidents of the family and the young, while ethical and moral problems arising out of the familial relationship were within the ecclesiastical jurisdiction. The American legal historian Professor Julius Goebel comments that "the common law first comes to grips with family problems in relation to the land, and for a long time this remains the major point of contact." It was typical of the older common law's unsentimental attitude that it fixed the age of majority at twenty-one, not because it considered that age the threshold of emotional maturity and responsibility, but because that was when a young man was considered sufficiently grown to carry the weighty equipment of a medieval warrior. The trend to transfer jurisdiction of marriage and the family to the temporal courts, which started with Henry VIII, was about completed by the temporary abolition of the ecclesiastical courts by the Commonwealth. The New England colonies, amenable to Puritan influences, considered the marriage status as a secular matter almost from the beginning.

Divorce, annulment, support, custody and the welfare of children have been matters of judicial concern and jurisdiction throughout the American experience. But the first move in the direction of a specialized court and judicial personnel for the handling of family problems was the proposal by the Chicago

Bar Association in 1899 for the enactment of a juvenile court act. According to that Association, "the fundamental idea of the law is that the State must step in and exercise guardianship over a child found under such adverse social or individual conditions as develop crime . . . It proposes a plan whereby he may be treated, not as a criminal or one legally charged with crime, but as a ward of the State, to receive practically the care, custody and discipline that are accorded the neglected and dependent child, and which, as the act states, 'shall approximate as nearly as may be that which should be given by the parents.' "

It was logical, as well as historical, that the growth of juvenile or children's courts to deal with problems of juvenile delinquency was followed by family or domestic relations courts to deal in large measure with the causes of delinquency—neglect, desertion, abandonment, nonsupport, paternity disputes and other conditions resulting from broken homes. In 1910 a Domestic Relations Division was created in the City Court of Buffalo, and in 1913 the Cincinnati Court of Domestic Relations was established with a view to combining in one court the functions of a domestic relations and juvenile court. These are the forerunners of the new judicial agencies hopefully assigned to absorb and resolve the cataclysmic social derangements reflected by the increase of 175 percent in delinquency referrals to juvenile courts between 1948 and 1958, the rise of 35 percent in divorce rates since 1950 (so that one in four new marriages today results in divorce) and the trebling of illegitimacy rates in the last two decades.

Juvenile and family courts—and civil and criminal courts to the extent that they affect children or the family unit—are fast taking on the coloration of social problem courts rather than courts of law. Children, and often youths and their parents, are assisted and not prosecuted, treated and not punished by such courts. As one writer puts it, the search is for "redemption, not retaliation." To this end the trend is quickened toward the use of highly specialized tribunals—children's courts, family courts, domestic relations courts—with their attendant personnel of social workers and psychologists. This body of experts will develop increasingly the data bearing upon issues of fault, or, more accurately, "cause"; and relief, or, more precisely, "therapy"—a function which is, of course, performed in the field and not in the courtroom. Fact-finding is thus shifted from the courtroom with its adversary process and rules of evidence, to the home, office, and neighborhood, with the nonjudicial mode of inquiry employed by the social sciences. In many jurisdictions today, important aspects of custody, adoption, guardianship and support proceedings, together with sentencing and juvenile procedures, involve the use of investigations and reports by probation officers and other social workers. The extensive use by courts of extrajudicial investigative reports reflects the tendency toward the "individualization" of treatment of litigants whose problems evoke consideration of social values.

Not only outside the courtroom, but in certain courtrooms proper, particularly in the juvenile courts, the procedures bear no close resemblance to the customary judicial form. A commentary by the National

Probation and Parole Association to one section of the latest version of the Standard Juvenile Courts Act notes:

> Whereas criminal court procedure is governed strictly by rules of evidence . . . the hearing in the juvenile court is much more informal, with greater flexibility governing the admission of evidence, and a far greater control by the judge over cross-examination and the order of presentation of evidence. The hearing is designated as informal, rather than summary as stated in a few juvenile courts acts. In addition, it is distinguished from the criminal court by the exclusion of the general public . . . The hearing should have the character of a conference, not a trial.
>
> The statutory direction on informality in children's cases has been erroneously interpreted in some juvenile courts as authorization to the judge to omit informing the persons before the court of their right to an attorney; in some instances this misinterpretation of informality has led the court to discourage—and even prohibit—attorneys' attendance at the hearings.

The judicial discouragement of counsel in juvenile court proceedings may, according to Professor Paulsen of Columbia Law School, be due to still another cause:

> It is probably true that few members of the bar operate easily in a non-adversary kind of proceeding, particularly in juvenile cases which seem much like ordinary criminal trials.

My own reading of a large number of juvenile court records makes plain the unhappy role that many lawyers play in juvenile cases. Often the attorneys are merely uninformed pettifoggers.

The described unorthodoxies of juvenile and family court procedures have not been unchallenged. Judge Olney of California declared that the juvenile court is "fast developing into a complete system of fascism, as dangerous to our institutions as communism." The Court of Appeals of New York has just recently vouchsafed the constitutional right to counsel, confrontation and cross-examination in those phases of a juvenile proceeding which determine whether the youngster is guilty of the charged delinquency. Other courts have sustained on constitutional grounds the juvenile's right to bail.

In 1955 a Family Part was established in the Supreme Court for New York County. The Part was supplied with two highly qualified social workers furnishing auxiliary services. The operations of the Part were studied by a special committee of the Association of the Bar of the City of New York, which pointed out that each of the judges assigned to the Part had been troubled by the use which should be made of the extrajudicial investigative reports of the social worker. It was noted that the "report is not sworn. It may contain extremely intimate personal revelations, along with statements and opinions of persons who are not parties. Its conclusions are a matter of opinion based on her [the social worker's] own insight into the character of the parties, and, particularly in a custody case, into the relative fitness of the parties for the custody of the children." Subsequently, in a case involving the custody of a ten-year-old, the New York Court of Appeals held that, except when otherwise stipulated, the social worker's report or psychiatric reports furnished to the social worker bearing on the issue of custody could not be received by the court in confidence and without disclosure to the parties or their lawyers. In so ruling the court followed similar decisions in Oregon, North Carolina, California and Indiana.

In the main, however, the techniques of juvenile and family courts have gone unchallenged and, when challenged, have been judicially approved. Judge Paul W. Alexander of the Toledo, Ohio, Division of Domestic Relations writes that in over forty thousand domestic relations and children's cases ranging over twenty years in his court, not a single attorney objected to the use of extrajudicial investigation reports: "In less than one case in hundreds does the lawyer bother to exercise his right to cross-examine the court worker." Thus, the extrajudicial investigations conducted by our family and juvenile courts often invade the private lives of children and adults in a fashion that would never be tolerated in a court handling litigation of a purely adversary nature. And indications confirm the future widening of the breaches already made in the walls of the juvenile and family courtroom through which evidence packaged outside is delivered and accepted in a form that would stamp it as contraband in conventional courtrooms.

Our canvass of the extent to which disputes in American society are no longer litigated in courts or by traditional judicial processes is not intended to be critical. The changes we have noted are principally for the better, and King Canute long ago demonstrated the futility of trying to shout down history. But it is timely to see and to state how far reality deviates from the American myth that a prescribed mode of trial, with all the protections of the Bill of Rights, is available when controversy remains unresolved or when government threatens personal freedom. It is no less timely to ask whether the inevitable continuance of the discernible trend away from the courts and their complement of judges, juries, lawyers, advocacy and rules of evidence and procedure will not just as inevitably erode the integrity of the trial process as we know it today.

What is involved is not only the future migration of still more business from the court's domains, but the contagion of indifference, at times approaching disdain, for the forms of the judicial trial. How long will the guarantees of the trial process remain vital if other processes, dealing with comparable problems, demonstrate the dispensability of those guarantees? If arbitration can do very well without lawyers, and administrative adjudication can function effectively while receiving hearsay, how long can the judicial trial continue to be unaffected by such experience? And if loyalty-security, deportation, denaturalization, denationalization and civil service tenure proceedings can go forward without confrontation of witnesses and without the fullest protection of each of the provisions of the Bill of Rights, how long can it be expected that the rights of an accused in a criminal trial will remain unchanged?

CHAPTER FIVE

THE JURY

IN CHARACTERISTIC AMERICAN STYLE, trial by jury is formally revered and informally satirized. *The Federalist No. 83,* said to have been written by Alexander Hamilton, tells us that the Founding Fathers at the Constitutional Convention concurred "at least in the value they set upon the trial by jury," the less enthusiastic regarding it "as a valuable safeguard to liberty," others representing it "as the very palladium of free government," and all being "satisfied of the utility of the institution, and of its friendly aspect to liberty."

Mr. Dooley's comment on trial by jury is, as might be expected, somewhat more mordant:

> Whin the case is all over, the jury'll pitch th' tistomony out iv the window, an' consider three questions: Did Lootgert look as though he'd kill his wife? Did his wife look as though she ought to be kilt? Isn't it time we wint to supper?

Revered or satirized, the use of the jury to find and announce the truth is a prominent feature of the American trial process which directly confronts the forces of change in American society and technology.

As we use the term jury here it refers to a group of laymen who, in a court trial, resolve issues of fact and then, applying the judge's charge or instructions on the law to the facts, determine which litigant is entitled to prevail. The invariable and key attributes of the modern jury are its impartiality and transiency. The jury, in each case, is a representative but different panel of laymen wholly disassociated in interest from either side in the case.

In one of his short plays William Saroyan writes of a set of jurors who, at a command, switch places with the accused. Saroyan's artifice is disturbingly valid. The litigant of today is the juror of yesterday or tomorrow. Litigants usually, and jurors almost always, are laymen, indistinguishable in their disassociation from the established law system. Like most litigants, jurors come from among the governed, and are distinct only in that while functioning as jurors they are temporarily among the governing.

The jury as fact-finder is not merely performing a pragmatic function in our democracy. The jury represents one of the most deeply imbedded facets of the American legal mythology. The United States Constitution originally provided that "the trial of all crimes, except in cases of impeachment, shall be by jury." And when the coverage under this guarantee was found inadequate, the Bill of Rights added, as part of the Seventh Amendment, that "in suits at common law, where the value in controversy shall exceed twenty dollars, the right of trial by jury shall be preserved." Every state has the requirement of a jury trial for serious criminal charges, and most states afford the right to bring before a jury "suits at common law"—usually actions for money damages. Yet, as we shall see, neither the authority nor the widespread use that the American jury system still retains can promise it immunity from the impact of the population growth, the computer, the public opinion poll and the heightened efficiency of related disciplines.

The principal historical origin of the Anglo-American jury came by way of an ingenious import. The Norman conquerors needed an effective system for gaining accurate and current information on the holdings and doings of their Saxon subjects. Plainly the best, cheapest and most readily available source for such essential intelligence was the Saxon community itself. For this purpose the ancient Norman inquest was adapted, requiring "jurors" to report to the king or to his representatives the juror's knowledge of communal matters of interest to the administration. The early significance of the juror's knowledge of such facts, to be reported by him upon his oath, is shown by the derivation of the word juror from the French *juré*, meaning sworn.

In time the device of the jury became the instrumentality for the displacement of private, local and feudal procedures with a centralized system of king's justice. Private accusation, in the form of the ancient appeal of the individual or the revenge-motivated hue and cry of the victim's kinship group, gave way to the grand jury presentment and indictment; ritualistic trials in local or feudal tribunals yielded to trial by jury in the king's courts. The grand jury evolution followed so soon upon the Norman Conquest in 1066 that by the end of the twelfth century the first great English legal tract by Glanville spoke of the system of accusation "by the public voice." By the fourteenth century the grand jury had attained such stature that it was provided that "from henceforth none shall be taken by petition or suggestion made to our lord the King, or to his council, unless it be by indictment or presentment of good and lawful people of the same neighborhood where such deeds be done."

Trial as well as accusation by jury similarly developed as strong medieval English kings, successors to William the Conqueror, struggled to establish the royal hegemony. In the twelfth century Henry II made trial by jury available in his courts for a variety of land controversies. When Pope Innocent III condemned trial by ordeal in 1214, the growth of trial by jury was accelerated so that it became the common mode of trial in criminal as well as civil cases by the end of the reign of Henry III in 1272.

As the jury system was extended in the thirteenth century to the trial of issues of fact, however, the jury continued to be selected from the vicinage or neighborhood and consisted of men with personal knowledge about the matter being litigated. The jury's job was to render a verdict on their knowledge of the case garnered prior to trial, and not in the courtroom. Today, of course, a juror who acquired any evidence outside of the courtroom would be disqualified, on the theory that such evidence had not been tested and verified in the truth-finding crucible of the court processes.

Once fact-finding was left to the community, the rise of the jury "as the very palladium of free government" was set in motion. For when a tyrant undertook a program of oppression he was obliged to bring his victim before a jury of laymen more closely identified with victim than oppressor. Thomas Erskine, only recently described by Lord Birkett as "the greatest advocate who ever practiced at the English Bar," was among the lawyers in England and the North American colonies who courageously and artfully exploited the sympathy of juries for those who were charged with sedition, treason and libel, although guilty only of harboring or expressing ideas distasteful to the Establishment.

Great and ancient as is the institution of trial by jury, it is not impervious to change. England, the cradle of the jury, now entertains less than two hundred jury trials a year in civil cases—no more than 2 to 3 percent of the total number of trials. It virtually abolished the jury in the trial of civil cases in 1933. Lord Evershed, Master of the Rolls of Great Britain, said of this development recently that "the change is largely attributable to the effects of two world wars and their pressure on all the available energies of our man-power."

Opponents of the jury system here are encouraged by the fact that there is now general agreement that the English experience has proven eminently successful and that bench, bar and public in England seem fully satisfied. Other considerations promise an acceleration in the near future of demands that this country follow the English lead in confining trial by jury in civil actions generally to defamation and similar complaints. Any fair estimate of the likelihood of our continuance of the jury system requires a comprehensive review and appraisal of the reasons proffered for and against trial by jury today.

Of course, few seriously advocate abolishing the jury in criminal cases. Even the most hard-bitten critic will either concede the unique value of the jury in criminal matters, or grudgingly admit that the public would never stand for its elimination where life and liberty are at stake. A powerful school believes that in a criminal case only the jury can bring the compassion of the community into the courtroom and soften for some particular defendant the harshness of laws designed to regulate human conduct in general. Over the years, the jury, primarily in the criminal case, has become, in the hearts and minds of many people, a bulwark against bureaucracy and against arbitrary, biased or corrupt action by judges.

But a campaign to eliminate the jury in civil cases has currently taken on fresh vigor. Lawyers and judges in this country are deeply concerned with our apparent inability to stem the mounting tide of ever-increasing delay in the courts; and jury critics attribute much of this delay and needless expense to the time wasted by the jury function. A reaction to this concern was manifested in California recently when Governor Edmund G. Brown, in an annual message, invited study of a plan to take automobile accident cases out of the courts, to be processed in an administrative bureau, as are claims in workmen's compensation. This would, for better or for worse, resolve the jury problem in auto accident cases—about 50 percent of all the cases in the courts.

There are some American courts—for example, in Cook County, Illinois, and Nassau County, New York State—where the delay in reaching trial after an answer has been filed by a defendant is over five years. Recent statistics supplied by the Institute of Judicial Administration disclosed that the average de-

lay between the filing of an answer and the jury trial
of a personal injury case was 13.3 months in the nation's state courts—an average which increases with
the size of the community, reaching 22.6 months in
counties of more than 750,000 and 29.6 months
throughout the State of New York. Of course, delays
of such length can mean substantial deprivation of
justice; and they invite a dangerous loss of public
confidence in the courts.

The average jury trial in the Supreme Court of
New York County takes four days. It has been estimated that this is two and one-half times as long as
the time required to try a similar case without a jury.
While the statistic has been challenged, it is clear
that the nonjury trial is much shorter. The hours
spent in the selection of a jury, opening and closing
statements to the jury, the judge's charge, all take
time; and there are the time-consuming histrionics
which lawyers fondly believe are so necessary before
a jury.

It is claimed that jury trials not only waste time,
but also money. The cost to the taxpayers is $3,000 a
trial in the Supreme Court of New York County, at
the rate of $750 a day for the maintenance of one
courtroom and its complement of judge and court
officers. There is also an enormous loss of manpower.
In the City of New York alone over half a million
man days are devoted to jury service each year.

The present considerable cost of jury trial in civil
actions is only an augury of things to come if juries
continue to try actions to recover money damages for
personal injuries, property loss and breach of contract. The greater part of civil litigation in the
United States—90 percent, it has been estimated—

involves claims for personal injuries caused by the negligence of another.

We are gaining about 250,000 new Americans a month. Litigation keeps pace with population and the increased use of accident-inducing appliances. Studies have shown that the New Jersey court calendar caseload rose 42 percent between 1949–50 and 1957–8; civil cases filed in Connecticut increased from 8,273 in 1950 to 13,804 in 1959; California's Superior Courts had 106,000 new civil cases in 1955 and 127,200 in 1958; while in the Counties of New York and the Bronx 44,000 statements of retainers in personal injury cases were filed by lawyers in 1957, and 66,000 were filed in 1959. Judge J. Edward Lumbard of the Court of Appeals for the Second Circuit has noted the dilemma of the state courts in handling accident cases: "The faster they bail out their boat the faster the water rushes in. In the thirteen years from 1942 to 1955, a population increase of 22 percent, drivers' licenses increase of 49 percent, motor vehicle registration increase of 78 percent, and a motor vehicle accident increase of 163 percent tell us the flood will increase."

Beyond question our present rate of growth, both of technology and of population, will soon make it necessary to find some workable means to accommodate the onslaught of civil litigation. Our present judicial plant is inadequate in numbers and equipment for the purpose. And since trial by jury is demonstrably slow and costly, the institution will surely be closely re-evaluated to see whether it should continue to serve the brave but busy new world of the future. In any such re-examination of the jury trial in civil cases we may expect as the most serious over-all criticism that the jury is less competent and less efficient than the judge as a fact-finder. On the other hand, if the jury is more effective in its present province than the judge, then it could be argued very impressively that the quality of justice should not be diminished by budgetary considerations, and that the obvious answer to court congestion is to provide more judges, more courthouses and more courthouse personnel.

One familiar complaint is that lawyers sedulously exclude the most competent members of a panel from actual jury duty. Indeed, a well-known trial lawyer who represents plaintiffs in accident cases has written that married men and women favor plaintiffs; experts, professional people, nurses and wives of professionals are to be avoided, because they are indifferent to pain and suffering and inclined to rely on their own learning; and accountants are to be shunned, for they may inform their fellow jurors of the tax immunity afforded judgments for personal injuries.

A famous prosecutor told one of the authors he would never select a man with a beard as a juror, as he had found they were nonconformists and would, in an open-and-shut case, hold out and hang a jury out of sheer cussedness. And so, ad infinitum, lawyers have their pet notions and techniques for excusing jurors, irrespective of their competence—in fact, frequently because of such competence. Again, statutory exemptions from jury duty relieve millions of our best-qualified citizens from serving.

A variation of this theme is that the average jury lacks the training and capacity to understand and determine a disputed set of complicated facts. Efficient and admirable as they may be in their various

callings, the argument runs, jurors are seldom trained
and disciplined to remain mentally alert throughout
long and sluggish court sessions. A judge, on the other
hand, is conditioned continuously to keep his eye on
the ball all through a trial, to find the true facts and
apply the applicable rules of law to those facts. Also,
a judge sitting without a jury is usually required to
make what are known as findings of facts—that is, to
furnish a statement, in some detail, of every important fact upon which he bases his ultimate decision.
But a jury typically renders what is called a general
verdict—an inscrutable "guilty" or "not guilty" verdict, or one for so many dollars in damage. There can
be no peering behind the countenance of this verdict
to ascertain how the jury decided the separately con-
tested issues of fact, or whether it followed the judge's
instructions on the applicable law.

There is the familiar contention that very often the
judge's charge is unintelligible to the jury or, even
when thoroughly understood, is deliberately disre-
garded. "Lawless jurors," as Roscoe Pound terms
them, will knowingly refuse to follow the judge's
instructions because they believe the particular law
to be unjust or silly or unfair. Each time a jury dis-
regards the law it constitutes itself a little legislature
and legislates within the jury room. The legal
logicians believe that given a set of facts the law
should be predictable, and the jury lawlessness de-
stroys such predictability. They also point out that
laws are made for the long run, and juries can bring
dangerous, short-lived popular passions and prejudices into the courtroom.

John Dryden has touched on this jury tendency in
verse:

> *The man who laughed but once, to see an ass*
> *Mumbling to make the cross-grain'd thistles pass;*
> *Might laugh again, to see a jury chaw*
> *The prickles of an unpalatable law.*

The pragmatists among the jury critics point not only to the apparent success of the English experiment in virtually abolishing jury trial in civil cases, but argue that in actual practice vast numbers of equity cases in both England and America have for centuries been tried before a judge alone. A judge sitting alone in an equity case can grant such drastic and varied relief as the rescission, reformation or specific performance of a contract, injunctions, foreclosure of mortgages, marital separation and custody of children. A judgment in an equity case can often affect the lives and fortunes of litigants much more vitally than a judgment for money damages only. Still, there has been no agitation to introduce juries into equity trials. And so the jury critics conclude that deference to the jury system is just a manifestation of hidebound allegiance to outworn tradition.

The really critical question, therefore, into which most of the complaints about the jury system funnel, is whether over-all the judge or the jury is best qualified to determine where the truth lies in a trial and to make an appropriate decision on the basis of that determination.

The defenders of the jury have no hesitancy in locking horns with its critics on this threshold but important question. They can quote many judges in praise of the composite acumen, conscientiousness, fairness and balance of juries. Professors Harry Kalven, Jr. and Hans Zeisel, directors of a number of massive surveys conducted by the Jury Project of the University of Chicago Law School, have written us that on the basis of their varied research their current impression is that the jury understands and retains enough of the evidence to do its job. They make the point that it is not necessary that every juror recall each item of evidence accurately. It is sufficient if a few jurors do so, as "the collective recall and intelligence of the jury is far higher than the average recall and intelligence of the individual juror."

It is pointed out that judges as well as jurors can be excessively emotional, biased, prejudiced or even unintelligent. The danger is that such a failing in a judge can decide a case, while in a juror its virulence will be diluted among all twelve members of the jury. Perhaps G. K. Chesterton had this in mind when he said, "I would trust twelve ordinary men, but I cannot trust one ordinary man."

"Lawless jurors," it is contended, may not fully appreciate all of the influences that affect their decisions—but neither does a judge. And it is argued that it is healthy for jurors to require that a law square with community notions of fair play.

Perhaps it is the fear of encountering what could prove to be the conclusive although honest bias in a judge or perhaps it is the too rigid application of the law which contributes to the public distrust of trial before a one-man tribunal. In October 1957 the American Institute of Public Opinion announced the results of a survey of adults on the subject of judges and juries. To the question "Suppose you were accused of committing a not-too-serious crime—would you rather be tried before the local judge or before a jury?" the answer was:

Before a judge   35%
Before a jury   51%
Don't know   14%

On the question of the alleged superiority of judges in the fact-finding process, a study conducted several years ago by the University of Chicago Law School group found that about 500 state and federal judges agreed in large measure with jury verdicts— in about 80 percent of the cases—in a testing of about 3,000 criminal and personal injury cases tried before them. The same study group made a survey of the judiciary on judges' basic attitudes toward the jury system, asking whether its disadvantages outweigh its advantages so much that its use should be sharply curtailed. The preliminary results show that only 3 percent of the judges thought that the use of the jury should be thus curtailed in criminal cases, and only 6 percent thought it should be in civil cases.

Perhaps it is the judges who should be commended for agreeing with the juries. The jurors bring the sentiment and sense of the street into the courtroom; and it is the street that ultimately makes the law that judges perhaps too long immured in ivory towers must enunciate and follow. Again, each term of service is a fresh and widely separated experience for a juror. Fact situations that have become routine to the judge through depressing similarity in case after case, and which he may come to adjudicate in routine fashion, are new and challenging to the juror.

The jury as a group, its champions submit, may be entertained but will not be influenced by a lawyer's wiles. And while a lawyer may sometimes try to exclude an intelligent and competent juror, he cannot carry that practice very far. The number of peremptory challenges—the outright exclusion of jurors for which no reason need be given—is limited. Usually a jury can be obtained which will fairly and faithfully reflect a cross-section of the community, in intelligence as well as the other virtues and failings.

As we have seen, the Founding Fathers took great pains to spell out in the Constitution the absolute right to grand jury and petit jury in criminal prosecutions and to petit jury in civil cases in federal courts; similar provisions are found in state constitutions for state courts. This was one way of assuring that the trial process would never be turned over to a bureaucracy that might become too subservient to governmental power, or too obsessed with the letter of the law at the expense of higher human values. The jury introduces into the trial process a fresh, constant stream of uncommitted, undogmatic transients with no hardened preconceptions, no grouping by types, no vested interest or convictions as to the outcome of the litigation. And underneath all this there are still vestiges of the feeling that the little fellow opposed by powerful interests fares better at the hands of a jury of his peers.

Therefore, as previously indicated, it is urged by jury champions that while jury trials may be more expensive and more protracted than nonjury cases, these are the proper governmental costs of continuing and assuring to the public a confident sense of justice. There can be no risking the inferior administration of justice because of additional expense. The jury protagonists also suggest the exploration of other remedies within our present procedure, such as broader and streamlined pretrial disclosures, elimination of the requirement for unanimity of the jury in rendering a verdict, perhaps the taxing of additional jury costs against the losing litigant to discourage the practice of demanding a jury as a tactical delaying device, a six-man jury or separate trials on the issues of liability and damages.

The jury system has been a visible, close-at-hand symbol of democracy. In both civil and criminal cases it affords our citizens an opportunity to participate directly in the processes and responsibilities of government—a participation that has been decreasing steadily in our highly complex and urban society. We were reassured recently that, despite the economic and other hardships involved, citizens appreciated this opportunity to participate. In 1957 a questionnaire was distributed, designed to obtain the reactions of a substantial number of persons who had recently served as jurors in the Supreme Court of New York County. In answer to one question 57 percent termed their jury service a worthwhile experience, 10 percent a pleasant duty, 23 percent a necessary but not too pleasant duty, 9 percent pretty much a waste of time, and 1 percent a very unpleasant experience. In answer to what they liked about jury duty, 38 percent responded by indicating the participation in a civic duty and 35 percent chose observing democracy in action.

If the jury is eliminated in the far more numerous civil cases, we may forget the significance of the jury in the defense of criminal charges. In one or two generations memories of the priceless heritage of trial by one's peers might be dimmed, and the jury system consigned to the limbo of outworn expedients, like the trial by battle or ordeal of several centuries ago. Sir Patrick Devlin has called the jury the "lamp of freedom." We would not want to risk the darkness of tyranny because of lack of oil for the lamps of freedom. For we suspect that no one can know whether the jury system will be missed unless and until there comes a period of crisis—when it will be most needed—and then there will be too little time to restore it. Trial by jury could be a most effective weapon in democracy's arsenal to combat the tyranny that cannot emerge until it has effectually overridden the right of the individual to raise his voice, first in the legislature and then in the courtroom.

We would cling to the jury system although fully aware that it will soon face its sternest test, beside which the attacks outlined previously in this chapter will appear puny. The assault upon the jury as a fact-finding unit has not as yet mounted the siege guns offered by modern science and modern disciplines. The controversy has thus far been limited largely to the relative merits of the jury as opposed to decision-making by the judiciary alone. In another chapter we have discussed the promise offered by narcoanalysis to recall and reveal the truth uncontestably in the laboratory, or at least more effectively than in the courtroom under present-day litigation rules. If narcoanalysis and a number of scientific techniques now in various stages of development fulfill their sponsors' anticipations, a new and most formidable element will enter the jury's struggle for survival. The issue will no longer be whether judge or jury can perform the fact-finding function more satisfactorily. Rather, it will lie between the courtroom, with its acquired accommodations to the strengths and frailties of society and individual, and the un-compromising out-of-court scientific agency.

Can scientific techniques temper cold justice as written in the statutes with the alleviating community biases reflected in jury action? Let us take a fairly common type of case in the criminal courts. A group of male teenagers, who in morals and intelligence reflect their average age level in the community, spy a neighbor's car in his driveway, with the key in the ignition lock. Somebody, in a spirit of derring-do, or from an excess of animal spirits, suggests they take a ride in it. Not wishing to lay themselves open to the most devastating charge in the teenage lexicon— that of "chickening out"—the others agree impul-sively, pile into the car, and in a short time smash it up.

They are arrested and charged with what the of-fense calls for according to the statute books—the very serious felony of grand larceny. Juries, in their wisdom, have over the generations recognized the transgression for what it really is—the theft of a ride rather than a car; and prosecutors have found it extremely difficult to obtain convictions in such cases. Therefore, wise judges and district attorneys, antici-pating jury reactions, usually reduce such charges to the offense of disorderly conduct or to the misde-meanor of petit larceny.

It remains to be seen whether the scientific tech-niques can winnow the gross crime from the less consequential offense, when both have the same statutory stature, upon the basis of such factors as age and background of the offender, real intent, morally pardonable motivations, rarely encountered and legislatively unanticipated temptations and the like. And if science is unable to make such distinctions, should such considerations of compassion yield to the desirability of impregnable fact-finding?

No matter how the jury system fares against attacks based upon the needs of economy and efficiency, it will surely be affected by the new science of electronics. At a conference sponsored jointly by the American Law Institute and the American Bar Association in Washington during March 1961, lawyers and technicians peered into the future to discuss "A Preview of Some Legal Problems Ahead in the Use of Electronic Data Processing in Business, Industry and Law." The initial discussion told of the conference's concern "with the informational content of coded ripples in a mercury puddle, a minutely magnetized ferrite donut, a magnetic pattern on a coated plastic ribbon, a spread of perforations on a paper tape." Quite correctly a speaker noted that "it is hard to find someone in our contemporary society who is not somehow involved in designing, building, selling, buying or using computers, or being 'processed,' paid, recorded, served, harassed, or bedeviled by them. There has been a fantastic widening of application from the original problem of calculating artillery trajectories, as exemplified by the range of subjects at this conference." And yet the key activity in electronic processing of data was said to be "so new that it is not yet characterized by any single title; but it is commonly referred to as computer programming."

Formidable and esoteric as the electronic computer may be, its function can be stated as that of storing and then rapidly disgorging on signal vast quantities of information. Since the information stored is appropriately classified, the computer is capable of reporting data not only in the same sequence as the data was originally stored, but also together with other data similarly indexed. As the number of variables in the material fed the computer increases, the number of possible relationships which can be elicited from the machine rises geometrically almost to the point of infinity. Enough is revealed about the computer potential by the reminder of IBM's director of research communications, Arthur L. Samuel, that computers are being programed "to match pennies, play tic-tac-toe, play checkers and chess, write poetry, compose music, and solve high school problems in plane geometry"; a Columbia University scholar recently claimed, through the use of an electronic computer, to have solved a centuries-old problem of Greek literature—whether the *Iliad* was composed by one man.

The application of the computer to the law has lately been the subject of learned inquiries at the Health Law Center of the University of Pittsburgh, Western Reserve University School of Law and Center for Documentation and Communication Research, the Southwestern Legal Foundation and the UCLA and Yale Law Schools. A program for storing and retrieving judicial decisions is also reported in progress at the Leningrad State University in the Soviet Union, while George Washington University and a data processing concern have prepared a report for the Antitrust Division of the Department of Justice on electronic procedures to speed legal research in antitrust cases. Obvious uses of the computer are to be found in corporate, banking, patent and accounting phases of the law, which typically involve numerous transactions or items of information capable of manageable classification. In each of these areas the computer promises enormous economies of time and space in the correlation and recall of material. The legal profession is even now engaged in adapting rules of evidence, presently based upon the testimony of the live witness, to the testimony of the machine.

A more distinctive use of the computer in the judicial process derives from the importance of authority or precedent in the American method of decision. Where a valid statute points the way to decision, a court is bound to follow no matter what might be the court's own view of the wisdom of the legislative mandate. And where a prior judicial decision on an identical or closely analogous situation exists, that decision governs if rendered by a higher court until expressly negated because of obsolescence or change of law. Because of this conclusive quality of the applicable statute or decision in American law, much of the business of advocacy and decision-making involves a squirrel-like search and hoarding and strategic use of nuggets of articulated authority. One of the familiar images of the lawyer at work is the library-entombed, bent-over figure, capped with a green eyeshade, surrounded by old, leather-bound law volumes and enscribbled pads of legal foolscap— a figure who suddenly snaps to an erect and fulfilled position and mutters "Eureka" as he finally dislodges from an entire library the solitary but indisputable prize for which he has been prospecting.

It requires no great imagination to envision how the computer can substitute a clean, rapid and impersonal process for the romantic image of the lawyer as tracker of the law. The principles of electronic processing of data plainly lend themselves to the organization, retention and recall of statutes and decisions along lines of classification even now used in the indices and digests which provide the starting point for most current legal research. No doubt it will still remain for lawyer and judge to evaluate and appraise the raw data to be supplied on a given point by the machine. But the legal research computer is at the very least the future vehicle for assuring complete coverage of appropriate authority. And such assurance will probably extend to the small lawyer as well as the great law firm as relevant sections of entire law libraries are made available to all through computers located at bar associations, law schools, courthouse libraries or law publishing services.

The prospect is that the brightly lit computer will serve in place of the bright young Harvard Law researcher for the moderate-income lawyer of the future. Judges, no less than lawyers, will welcome and use electronic research for expedition and uniformity. But, as has been remarked by Dr. Edward Teller, machines have "become teachable, acquire experience, form judgments, develop emotions and take initiative" and "any logical human process can be copied by the machine." One wonders whether a computer will be devised to take the next step into the realm of reason and policy, which begins where authority and precedents end, and thereby replace the judge, and the lawyer too in many of his functions.

To appreciate the likely impact of the computer upon the future of the jury, it must be remembered that today the jury is assumed to act as a cross-section

of the community. When a jury is asked to decide
which of conflicting lines of testimony is truthful, it
is supposed to do so by bringing to bear the com-
monsense attitudes and understanding attributed to
everyman. The jury functions even more directly as
vox populi when it is obliged to determine, as its
major preoccupation, whether a litigant acted as a
"reasonable" or a "prudent" or a "fair-minded" man
would. Such an issue is present in most trials, and
in almost all negligence case trials. The driver who
injures a pedestrian is liable in damages if he did not
operate the car as a "reasonable" man would in the
circumstances. Divining what a "reasonable" man
would do involves an inquiry, perhaps a species of
projection and self-inquiry on the part of the jury,
which is seldom a matter of proof. The jury, as the
community representative, is presumed to be, in the
aggregate, the mythical "reasonable" man.

Presently each jury recasts for itself its image of
the appropriate "reasonable" man. Undeniably this
means different results as juries, times and places
change. But uniformity of result in substantially like
circumstances is one of the desiderata of an ideal
system of justice. This is one of the significations of
the phrase "equal justice under law."

Functioning in conjunction with public opinion
polls, which explore and report today's community
views, computers would leave little basis for the
contention that the jury is the most efficient agency
to plumb the contemporaneous views of a community
in those cases where such views are an essential
ingredient of decision. Polls undertake to find and
articulate the sentiment of a community—one of the
functions attributed to the jury. In public opinion

polling the disciplines of psychology and statistics have collaborated to the point of gauging with considerable—though not infallible—sensitivity and precision the sentiment of the community on matters ranging from deodorants to presidents. Even the severest critics of polling methods would acknowledge the superiority of the polls to the jury in accurately reflecting the views of a community. The expert would justifiably consider one jury entirely too small a sampling for polling purposes to give any validity to its findings. Because of the current acceptance of the art of polling, traditional rules of evidence have already been breached to permit the use of public opinion polls to prove public confusion in unfair competition and trademark or patent infringement cases, public opprobrium in suits for defamation and public morality in obscenity and immigration cases. There is the further remote possibility that public opinion polls as to what is "reasonable" or "prudent" could be fed to an omnivorous computer on a variety of recurrent factual situations, particularly in personal injury cases, for appropriate re-evocation upon the jury trial.

Still another aspect of the jury function is subject to invasion by the computer. Juries fix damages in money actions. Such actions may entail, in the language of the law, liquidated or unliquidated damages. Damages are liquidated where the amount, if owed, is not in dispute, as where the action is to recover on a promissory note or a check of a definite sum. Damages are unliquidated when the amount owed is in dispute, as where the action is to recover for personal injuries. In such cases the damages include not only past expenses and loss of earnings, but also future expenditures and losses as well as the money equivalent for pain and suffering.

The jury obviously has little discretion in determining the amount of damages when they are liquidated. In the many cases involving unliquidated damages, however, the jury is required to consider all the relevant factors which go to compensate a claimant fully for his losses. The personal injury claim finds the jury evaluating not only the nature of the injury, but the age and health of the claimant, the permanence of the injury, the extent of the pain, his actual and prospective expenses and loss of income and other items of damage.

The calculation of damages does not, however, consist of an unmanageable number of variables. From the Code of Hammurabi to the latest workmen's compensation schedules men have been able to anticipate and fix rates of retribution or compensation for injuries. It seems clear that the modern computer could be programed at least to assist a jury in the fixation of damages. Working data for such a purpose could be supplied by prior jury experience or expert actuarial advice. Of course, any such development would rob personal injury trials of much drama, since presumably a computer could not be expected to experience tears or shudder at the sight of a crippled claimant or a vivid photographic demonstration of the claimant's original injuries. Again the imperturbability of the machine would replace the romance of the trial.

The ultimate question presented by the advent of the computer and other techniques is whether the efficiency and uniformity they offer justify the necessary attendant loss of human values. Trial by jury as we know it today will not be the most proficient mode of fact-finding tomorrow. If the jury trial, particularly in civil actions, is to persist in its present form it will be only because, better than impersonal and mechanical devices, it will serve to closet men in close personal give-and-take consideration of matters of importance. No machine can substitute for the profound emotional significance of confrontation by one's peers as jurors. And no machine can replace the experience and responsibility of a juror confronting the person he must judge. A society already highly mechanized and suffering from a dilution of meaningful interpersonal relationships cannot easily or lightly displace any fundamental aspect of the institution of the jury in favor of the poll or the computer. The jury remains one of the stoutest chains binding the citizen to the law, since it is one of the very few areas where the layman and not officialdom governs directly. The only certain answer we can perceive at this point is the need we stress throughout this book—to anticipate the upcoming conflict in basic values, so that the final answer reached is a product of reasoned judgment and not improvised in response to some transient exigency.

CHAPTER SIX

THE LAWYER

THERE ARE FEW more reassuring images in American folklore than the family-serving general practitioner. The family doctor and the family lawyer—constant, competent and as familiar and concerned with the secrets of the family as the secrets of their crafts— are stock characters in the idealized picture of the American family. Whether portrayed as a dessicated *i*-dotter and *t*-crosser, or as a chubby, cherubic one, the old-fashioned family lawyer commanded the complete confidence of every member of the family. He knew where the skeletons were hidden and had often helped stow them away in the closet, but he would never relinquish the key. He had helped the young 'uns out of school and college scrapes, their parents out of marital and business ones. Altogether a secure bastion of trustworthiness, whom no one envisaged as suffering anguished hours over his own family problems, or straining to meet his office overhead.

The actual family lawyer had one fundamental quality in common with the mythical one. He was trustworthy and merited the confidence reposed in him. And since the family lawyer has played so important a part in our society, and has been so comforting a figure to generations of Americans, it is important to realize that his tribe is diminishing and may soon be extinct.

The identity of the American lawyer is changing surely and radically as the general practitioner in the law has been steadily giving way to the specialist, who very often is a layman. The former vast precincts of the individual general practitioner have become fragmented into the special provinces not only of the lawyer expert in tax law, labor law, marital law, antitrust law, but also of the accountant, labor relations consultant, marital adviser, economist, social worker, sociologist, penologist and other expert competitors. The sum total of this irreversible, constantly accelerating shift of function is, strangely enough, an unarticulated importation into the structure of the American legal profession of characteristics associated with the more venerable and castelike English system.

Although many features of our American body of law have been patterned closely after English jurisprudence, the organic structures of the two bars have traditionally been dissimilar. The English bar is composed of barristers and solicitors. Only the barristers are privileged to appear in court to plead cases of any size or importance. Clients are referred to them by solicitors. The barrister has little communication with the client, except through the solicitors, even in the actual preparation of the case for trial. And, strangely enough, although the glorious and romantic figures of the English bar are barristers, it requires longer and more rigid training to become a solicitor.

The solicitor advises clients as to their legal rights, draws documents, organizes business enterprises—in short, is the legal adviser and guide in business and personal situations. It is the solicitor, not the barrister, who therefore has the warm, often personal relationship with the client enjoyed so frequently by American lawyers. In this respect, the American lawyer had a great deal in common with the English solicitor. But, because of the limitations the English system imposes upon the professional activities of the latter, he has never achieved the grandeur and stature of his American cousin. For, while the solicitor may be the confidant of his client, he is not the client's champion before judge or jury; nor, on the other hand, does the barrister get close enough to his client to identify with him emotionally. Because of his remoteness, the barrister usually champions a client's cause of action or defense rather than the client himself. The American lawyer, until recently at least, has been the confidant as well as the champion of his client, has enjoyed the intimacy as well as the glamor, a blending of roles which has contributed importantly to the unique position he has occupied in our society.

In recent years we have moved toward a splitting of the lawyer's functions along similar barrister-solicitor lines in America. With the decline of the old-fashioned, all-around lawyer, there have evolved in practice well-marked and seldom crossed boundaries between the office lawyer and trial lawyer; and even these precincts have proliferated into numerous specialties. As a result, the resemblance the American lawyer of today bears to his precursor of the nineteenth century is rapidly fading.

Until a couple of generations ago the American lawyer in general practice enjoyed the affection of the many families he served—much as the family doctor did—and at the same time commanded a special community respect because of education, discipline, training and intellect. Professor E. E. Cheatham has pointed out that "until the latter part of the nineteenth century the lawyer was almost the only expert in the field of human relations."

No doubt, despite this mingled affection and respect in personal and private relationship, the public image of the lawyer in America, as in other countries and in all ages, has often evoked hostility. The lawyer's function and discipline are forever provocative to those impatient for great change. Dean Roscoe Pound has observed that "every Utopia that has been pictured has been designed to dispense with lawyers." But history has documented the indispensability of the lawyer to the functioning of any complex social organism. If differences between men, or between the individual and his society, are to be resolved peaceably and rationally, lawyers, or a reasonable facsimile, must engineer the process. Hostility to lawyers, whether diffuse or intense, ultimately must yield, in varying degrees, to the values served by a lawyer class. Both France and Russia, in the wake of their revolutions, abolished the legal profession. But even revolutionary regimes needed laws, and then lawyers to interpret and serve as guardians of these laws. So, within a short time, the profession emerged again in both countries.

In this country, in pre-Revolutionary times the Regulars of North Carolina protested "that lawyers . . . are become a nuisance." In 1641 the Massachusetts Body of Liberties prescribed that every litigant could plead his own cause and, if he needed legal assistance, he was to give his counsel "no fee or reward for his pains." At various times, the lawyer class has been anathema to our agrarian and debtor classes, to the Jacksonian, Populist, muckraking and other movements seeking large reforms. Carl Sandburg expressed a valid aspect of American folklore when he asked, "Why does a hearse horse snicker hauling a lawyer away?" The same sentiment can be seen in a recent Gallup poll which showed lawyers lower in public esteem than either of the other two learned professions (medicine and the ministry), and also lower than engineers or professors.

But the balance of American history is heavily weighted on the side of the lawyer. For no profession, craft or, indeed, class has made a deeper imprint upon the history and ethos of our country than the lawyer, despite the fact that his discipline, which requires him to study and digest before acting, is very annoying to those who press for dramatic, immediate change. And since those who advocate change are usually the most colorful and articulate of the citizenry, they try to hold up the frustrating lawyer as a horrible archtype of cowardice, myopia and, worst of all, stuffiness. Dr. Johnson is quoted as saying that "he did not care to speak ill of any man behind his back, but he believed the gentleman was an attorney."

The lawyer's status on the American scene, nevertheless, was correctly defined by the historian Professor Henry Steele Commager when he wrote:

> The dignity, prosperity, and influence of the legal profession is one of the most striking phenomena of American culture. Surely in no other country have lawyers occupied a comparable position or played a comparable role. It is a tribute to the posi-

tion of the lawyer that no other profession has inspired such a literature, or such a mythology, as the legal. Lawyers are legendary characters, their careers and their arguments the very stuff of folklore . . .

The evidence in support of Professor Commager's appraisal is persuasive.

We may take for granted, of course, that in this country, dedicated as we are to the concept of constitutionalism, lawyers would predominate in political life. Twenty-four of forty-five at the First Continental Congress and thirty-four of fifty-five at the Constitutional Convention were lawyers. Jefferson, Patrick Henry, John Adams, Madison, Dickinson, Jay, Marshall and Livingston were trained in the law. All but nine of our presidents have had some exposure to legal training. Of those nine only two—Washington and Theodore Roosevelt—are generally deemed of the first rank as presidents. It has been calculated that between 1865 and 1948, more than 70 percent of our national cabinet members, 58 percent of our state governors, 72 percent of the United States Senate, and 64 percent of the House of Representatives have been lawyers.

Even more indicative of the immersion of the lawyer in the mainstream of American life is his role in our literature and mythology. Our literary inheritance includes innumerable treatments of the lawyer and the law to be found in Shakespeare, in whose plays one scholar has counted three hundred allusions to the law, in Trollope, Reade, Fielding, Scott, Balzac, Dickens, Dostoyevsky, Stevenson, Thackeray, Lamb, Galsworthy, Rabelais, Zola and scores

of other recognized authors of distinction. Professor
D. W. Brogan has suggested that, because of the
significant place of the lawyer in American life, the
first great American novel was *The Scarlet Letter,*
with its moving depiction of the legal process in
early New England. Nor is it accidental that, as remarked by Malcolm Cowley, "Erle Stanley Gardner,
Perry Mason's papa, with more than a hundred million copies of his various works printed" is "the best-
selling American of all time." Hardly a season of the
theater or cinema passes without a dramatization of
the lawyer or the trial process (in recent years, among
others, *Inherit the Wind, The Andersonville Trial,*
Witness for the Prosecution, the various plays about
Oscar Wilde, *Daughter of Silence, A Man for All*
Seasons).

Any reference to the printed reading matter—
books, magazines, newspapers—enjoying wide distribution in this country would show a constant
preoccupation with the lawyer and his functions,
particularly at trials (e.g., the McCarthy hearings, *The*
Caine Mutiny, Anatomy of a Murder, By Love
Possessed, The Just and the Unjust, the Mr. Tutt
stories by Arthur Train, Louis Nizer's best-seller,
My Life in Court). Prime television and radio time,
directed to millions, is regularly devoted to depicting,
with varying degrees of verisimilitude, the lawyer at
work (e.g., "The Defenders," "Perry Mason," "Sam
Benedict").

Again and again the lawyer and the trial process
are the literary symbols used to express the most
profound aspects of the human condition: the lawyer
as the alienated, judging and judged everyman in
The Fall and *The Stranger* by Camus; the law and its

procedures and personnel as the personification of everyman's guilt in Kafka's *The Trial;* the lawyer as the protagonist for fallible and mortal man in the great struggle between good and evil in Benét's *Devil and Daniel Webster;* the lawyer as the medium of expressing man's responsibility to preserve and conform to those institutions and relationships by which society functions in Cozzens' *By Love Possessed* and Wouk's *The Caine Mutiny.*

Moving from literature to history, we find the pantheon of heroes and giants in American mythology is on population ratio disproportionately stocked with lawyers—Jefferson, Madison, Adams, Brandeis, Darrow, Cardozo, Learned Hand. The most deeply moving figure in American history, Abraham Lincoln, remains forever cast in the image of the trial lawyer. The same Gallup poll which ranks the lawyer low in public regard finds the chief justiceship of the United States a more hallowed occupation than the presidency.

The common components of the venerated lawyer image are stature, wisdom derived from experience, and courage as counsel and champion for the individual client caught up in conflict. The myth is that the lawyer, endowed with such qualities, unreservedly commits himself and those qualities to the cause of the individual, even when society itself and its institutions are the adversary. This involves the closest possible identification and merger of lawyer and client, while the lawyer, at the same time, preserves apart and intact his professional obligations as well as his artful techniques adapted to that special discipline known as the trial.

It is the unique and curious nature of the lawyer-client relationship—the trained champion identified with, yet ethically and professionally separated from the individual client—which is at the heart of the great American lawyer myth. It is that relationship and, therefore, that myth which is irrevocably in the process of change. Today the great lawyer on the American scene is more nearly typified by the late John Foster Dulles than by Abraham Lincoln. To compare Dulles with Lincoln—with no intention to diminish the formidability of Dulles—is to tell, in short, the story of the change in the myth of the American lawyer since the Civil War.

It has become standard historical procedure to chart changes in American life by referring, in chronological order, to the views of pre-eminent foreign commentators on America. This technique is especially revealing in tracing the changing character of the American lawyer.

In his *Democracy in America,* the French magistrate-historian Alexis de Tocqueville noted early in the nineteenth century that

> In America there are no nobles or literary men, and the people are apt to mistrust the wealthy; lawyers consequently form the highest political class and the most cultivated portion of society . . . If I were asked where I place the American aristocracy, I should reply without hesitation that it is not among the rich, who are united by no common tie, but that it occupies the judicial bench and the bar.

The bench and bar at the time De Tocqueville wrote filled a vacuum created by the comparative lack of education among the people—a lack which has since been partly remedied. Aristocracy being a relative term, the closing of the gap diminished greatly the aristocratic caliber of the legal profession. Consequently, by the turn of the twentieth century, Lord Bryce, in *The American Commonwealth,* still found that "the lawyers best deserve to be called the leading class," but also noted that

> . . . education is so much more diffused than formerly, and cheap literature so much more abundant, that they do not stand so high above the multitude as they once did.

By 1948, Harold Laski, in *The American Democracy,* considered that ". . . the character of the profession has changed because the greatest rewards it can offer now come not to the lawyer who is an eminent advocate . . . but to the lawyer who devotes himself to advising the vast corporations and combines which now dominate American economic life."

American observers have been more devastating in describing the post-Civil War changes in the character of the bar. Woodrow Wilson, as far back as 1910, perceived and predicted the trend of the lawyer-client relationship in America, and his insights stand confirmed a half-century later. After extolling the role played by lawyers in the formation and growth of the nation, and remarking on the necessity that courts interpret written constitutions, he deplored the lack of lawyers to man those courts. He found that lawyers were no longer trained in constitutional law, "which is in the background, very vague and general." The new, prevailing types of lawyer were "not general counsellors of right and obligation," but specialists, who were being drawn into business. Wilson went on to find that the lawyer had "become part of the mercantile structure rather than part of the general social structure of our commonwealth as he used to be." Lawyers had left the world of general interests and "become narrowed to a technical function. . . . They do not bear the relation to the business of their neighborhoods that the family doctor bears to the health of the community in which he lives."

Adolf Berle wrote in the same vein for the *Encyclopedia of Social Sciences* about nineteen years ago. He lamented that while lawyers in this country originally possessed a social eminence not accorded businessmen, their significance waned as lawyers increasingly became the associates if not the hirelings of captains of industry. For Berle the advent of the modern corporation has made the lawyer "an intellectual jobber and contractor in business matters."

More recently, the late Professor C. Wright Mills, the sociologist, discussing the new middle classes in his book *White Collar,* made penetrating observations on the lawyer's place in the present social order. Writing specifically of lawyers, Mills said: "As the new business system becomes specialized, with distinct sections and particular legal problems of its own, so do lawyers become experts in distinct sections and particular problems, pushing the interests of these sections rather than standing outside the business system and serving a law which co-ordinates the parts of a society."

The entire development from the lawyer-friend-champion to the lawyer-business colleague-specialist is implicit in Judge Learned Hand's curt observation that ". . . in my own city the best minds of the pro-

fession are scarcely lawyers at all." Judge Hand's re-
mark has its roots in a fitting and traditional
coupling of the lawyer with courtrooms—as surely
as the architect is coupled with buildings and the
doctor with hospitals—and expresses the transition
in the last half-century from the courtroom lawyer
to the office lawyer, from the great lawyer to the
great law firm. An examination of the principal
causes of that transition will show that they promise
to accelerate, not abate, and from that likelihood
flow implications of consequence to the bar, to the
community and to all those for whom the lawyer-
friend-champion has been a comforting image as well
as a reality.

There can be no denying or reversing the profession's growing identification with the business community. Increasingly the profession manifests an
occupational tie with corporate, property and financial rights. The American Bar Association's recent
monumental study of the legal profession discloses
that "there is a close relationship between the incomes of lawyers, by states, and the incomes after taxes
of the corporations of the corresponding states," and
that "the size of the bar is best reflected in the
proportionate wholesale sales by state." The same
study revealed that ". . . the number of lawyers who
are serving a single corporation's interests is steadily
growing." As our society continues to develop institutional conglomerates, including labor organizations,
replete with power, status, wealth and legal problems,
we may expect the profession to continue to cluster
about these complexes.

The former function of guiding middle-class individual interests has thus become subordinated to the

deference more profitably paid to larger business interests. And the declining numbers of small businesses that form the middle class of the commercial world—due to merger, absorption, chain and branch outlet competition—intensify the possessiveness of big business in relation to legal services.

As appears from the American Bar Association's study, the average net income of the solo practitioner in 1948 was $5,759, while the average net income of a partner in a law firm with nine or more members vaulted to $27,246. The meaning of the fivefold discrepancy between the income of the solo practitioner and the member of the large firm is plain to read when it is remembered that the individual practitioner more typically services a small-business and middle-class individual clientele, while the more lucrative corporate business is handled by law firms or house counsel. It is, therefore, not surprising that the numbers of the solo practitioner, as well as the abilities that he can develop only from actual experience, are on the decline, giving point to the warning of Dean Willard Hurst that "samplings of people of modest income show that there is probably a large amount of legal counselling and service that people need but are not seeking. Especially, the samples show a very large amount of preventive work that is not being done."

A few generations ago the most successful and most acclaimed lawyers made their reputations, and a good part of their living, in the courtroom. The interests and activities of the clients whom they represented reflected the interests and activities of society itself. And these luminaries of the bar conducted themselves publicly as befitted their exalted position, much as the matinee idols of those days tried to behave so as to mirror the public's image of themselves. One wonders which came first—the image or the reality.

The financial rewards, as well as the glory, flowed then to the trial lawyer. Today, the large incomes are most often earned by the corporation lawyer, who usually strives to keep his client out of court. With few exceptions, the big money earners, aside from a small number of lawyers specializing in personal injury cases, are the senior partners in the large law firms, which may employ from fifty to one hundred lawyers.

Leviathan financial structures have necessitated the formation of leviathan law firms to serve their needs. Taxation and government regulation, as well as intracorporate matters, have generated such a variety of complex legal problems as to require a high degree of specialization. This has proven attractive because it is profitable. Indeed, as the aggregate number of written court opinions has risen from 10,000 in 1750 to 2,000,000 in 1950, and our legislatures grind out more than 30,000 new laws annually, specialization is almost inevitable. Surely, no single lawyer and no leisurely, old-fashioned law office possesses the specialized experience or capacity to handle the multifarious problems of big business or big labor. Harrison Tweed, a public-spirited, successful lawyer, recently cautioned attorneys to "overcome in their own minds and then eliminate from the minds of others the traditional concept that a lawyer can be all things to all clients." This was advice counseling realism rather than modesty.

At one time the lawyer was bigger than his client and the lawyer's leadership of clients prepared and inspired him for community leadership. His stature in the community derived from public confidence in his learning and practical wisdom. Now the most wonderfully endowed lawyer may represent a business complex so colossal and impersonal that no one individual can affect its course appreciably. Less and less will the practice of the law be an internship or proving school in public leadership.

When the lawyer represented every element in the community, that community formed his professional universe. The leadership qualities he possessed were asserted for the entire community, in politics, philanthropy, education and other communal activities. Today, the most talented of our lawyers may serve one corporate client or a number of such clients with identical interests, and they will constitute the relevant professional universe.

True, the importance of the modern lawyer is now displayed backstage, and anonymously, rather than in the spotlight, as formerly; but it can nonetheless be very influential. With lawyers acting as house counsel to mammoth corporations, sitting on their boards, seeping out of the law into corporate executive positions, it is clear that if big business has molded the legal profession as its handmaiden, the legal profession has also had a hand in shaping the character of big business.

Unlike the lawyer of yesteryear, who was called in by a business client occasionally to discuss a problem or draw a contract, many lawyers today are meshed right into the everyday functioning of corporations. Decisions involving trade agreements, launching of price wars, daring advertising campaigns, stock bonus plans, preferential carriage agreements and many others that are the warp and woof of modern business enterprise are seldom made without consulting house counsel or the law firm representing the corporation.

In fact, all the signs and portents indicate that the organization lawyer will fuse into the organization man. He will develop an institutional loyalty that will make his campus allegiances seem anemic; he will never sing solo, but only raise his voice in the institutional chorus. But in the grand and glorious annals of the bar, it has been through singing solo that its men of mark have gained their strength and courage, their color and character. Whether working for a large law firm or a large corporation, the lawyer of today is remote from the role which made the practice of law an exciting and zestful calling for the lawyer of yesterday; and he seldom so identifies with a client as to hold his hand before crisis, or to lament or rejoice afterward. He is not warmed by the respect, affection and gratitude of clients and clients' families, whom he has guided wisely and conscientiously.

Many lawyers today are on a professional assembly line. One checks a client's documents for tax perils, another for libel possibilities, others for labor, antitrust and all the other problems which may beset modern enterprise. Harvey Swados, commenting on those professionals who are "all-but-anonymous units in the firm's labor force," makes the pun that the difference between them and factory workers may be only one of degree. He very perceptively observes:

> . . . Surely we must now realize that the young attorney, clerking in a huge law factory, or the young business administration graduate, disappearing into the paternal embrace of the giant corporation, can

rarely get from his daily work the satisfaction—to say nothing of the thrill—that his father did.

Nor can a young lawyer so placed develop the same sturdiness and resourcefulness which made his father a many-dimensioned human being and a leader in his community.

It also remains to be seen whether the identification of the lawyer with big business will result in a loosening of professional ethics. The standards which lawyers set for themselves are high, and are rigidly enforced in most jurisdictions. Lawyers regard themselves as public servants, entrusted with the assertion and enforcement of the legal rights of every member of the public, and with the shouldering, too, of everyman's legal responsibilities. The profession explicitly regards itself as charged with protecting the public against overreaching or depredations by lawyers. It is, however, growing increasingly difficult for the lawyer to detach himself sufficiently from the competitive climate of his client to give the client objective ethical guidance.

The business orientation of the lawyer, and his consequent specialization in the service of compartmentalized financial structures, are, we have seen, a prime cause for the new look of the profession. Another and related cause is the general flight of the lawyer, as well as the public, from the courts. We discussed this phenomenon at length earlier. Here the decline in the use of the judicial trial is pertinent as it has contributed to the changing character of the American lawyer. The litigation which has brought color, glory and prestige to the legal profession is only a sometime thing for the institutions which attract so many of its ablest members. Counsel for the successful business firm avoids litigation as costly and time-consuming. Big corporations, for example, seldom sue one another for breach of warranty, specific performance or any of the variety of causes for which individuals or smaller companies usually go to court. Only when their very existence seems imperiled, as in antitrust or unfair competition suits, do they go to court.

The bench has candidly described the consequences to the bar of the shift of legal talent from the courtroom. Speaking in 1956 to the Association of the Bar of the City of New York, Chief Judge J. Edward Lumbard of the United States Court of Appeals for the Second Circuit said:

> . . . in all courts since the 1920s there has been a marked decline in the art of advocacy and in the quality of the lawyers' work in the trial and appellate courts. This is the other side of the high cost coin—with too high a cost to litigants, the lawyer's fee is not enough to justify the amount of time and effort which must go into careful and effective preparation of most cases.

> Judge Learned Hand tells of sitting with Judge Hough, and as he did not know the lawyers who were arguing before the court, he passed a note to Judge Hough, "Who are these lawyers?" To this Hough wrote back, "Just some law clerks sent up by those Wall Street swells to talk to boobs like you and me."

In a brief story that is it: the courtroom is the least profitable side of the practice of law. The exceptional anti-trust cases, tax cases and certain kinds of administrative proceedings only emphasize the fact that the courtroom is no longer the forum it was when the great controversies of the day were fought out there by the leaders of the bar. So today many of our best barristers are forced by economic facts to forego litigation and turn to more lucrative fields. As a consequence, many of our leading lawyers make it a point never to go to court if they can possibly avoid it.

The administrative process is now an irrevocable fact of life which will surely expand into new as well as within old areas of governmental regulation. Arbitration now accommodates a steadily growing number of commercial, labor and other controversies. It is clearly indicated that this informal procedure will be resorted to increasingly for the resolution of business disputes. But the most momentous long-term prospect for the legal profession is the likely eventual transfer of accident cases from courts to commissions and bureaus, as in the processing of workmen's compensation coverage for industrial injuries. We do not pause to discuss the weighty arguments that have been made for and against such a shift; we do not believe it is imminent; but it is a prospect which must be seriously considered. The nonsalaried and part-salaried lawyers engaged in private practice still receive more than 50 percent of their income from individuals, as compared with business clients. But the single practitioner, representing the majority of those lawyers earning income from individuals, depends heavily upon substantial—though contingent

—fees in personal injury cases to carry the marginal law work that is otherwise frequently derived from individual clients.

The Columbia Project for Effective Justice estimates that in New York City alone 190,000 accident victims collect $220,000,000 annually, of which $75,000,000 is paid out in legal fees. The removal of personal injury cases from the courts would eliminate the critical nourishment of a few large fees for many lawyers with small incomes. The loss of these fees, together with the other indicated inroads into the staples of present-day practice, would cause some lawyers to abandon the practice of law altogether and would mean an ever-increasing channeling of the activities of those remaining in the profession into the service of the business community.

The most substantial future contacts between the bar and the trial process as we know it which can be envisaged with some certainty will be in the representation of private rights entailing relatively modest economic interests. The court will still be resorted to when economic conflicts between groups erupt into antitrust, patent infringement, unfair competition or stockholders' suits, or into labor disputes. But in the main, litigation will be confined to criminal, matrimonial, surrogate and realty matters, property damage and collection suits, to proceedings involving organizational or institutional membership and judicial review of administrative action. These are the litigated problems principally of middle- and lower-income classes, and do not hold out to the profession the same financial and other rewards to be found in advising and counseling corporations and other institutions.

The evolving pattern is clear: courtroom advocacy demands skills, energies and time in preparation and trial, for which our society is not prepared to pay as much as it will for other legal activities. Litigation will increasingly be handled by the specialist, the beginner or the lawyer not otherwise more profitably occupied. All these factors are reflected in the reluctance of most law students to prepare for careers as trial lawyers, as opposed to the better-paying fields.

In sum, we may expect that the ranks of the general practitioners, who have been such a source of reliance and comfort to individuals and families, will diminish sharply in number and ability. The "best minds of the profession" will be drawn into advising the so-called power pyramids—giant corporations, unions and other institutions. They will also advise the individuals in the upper executive echelons on their private affairs. The lawyer-client relationship will become more transient and less enduring. It will also be less warm. For the lawyer who comes from the client's corporate, union or other institutional affiliation is not the client's own lawyer. He is an institutional lawyer, and rarely conveys to the client any feeling beyond that of clinical efficiency.

The trial champion, courageous and flamboyant, is being replaced by the safe grayness of the businessman-lawyer who would consider the trial work which occupied the great Darrow as professionally embarrassing, or as professionally bizarre—in any event, as professionally unprofitable. Who, then, will remain to wage the never-ending battle for the preservation of civil liberties, to defend the accused, to represent the underprivileged? Certainly not counsel supplied by the institutions, except possibly labor unions—

and there appears to be a tendency among labor unions to dispense with lawyers' services, particularly in negotiations. Perhaps a redefined and highly energized public defender system will fill the gap.

In his reminiscences Justice Frankfurter reflected that "a lawyer's life touches life at so many points. It's satisfying because if a lawyer is any good, he isn't the fellow the layman sees going into court on a pettifogging enterprise. A lawyer comes nearer being a priest and a psychiatrist in combination than any other profession. Like a family solicitor in England he not only attends to the business affairs of the family, but if there is domestic difficulty, or rows with a partner, he's a family advisor, and in the big cities he's a composer of difficulties and not just a wrangler in Old Bailey or in the Essex Market police courts."

Justice Frankfurter has drawn an appealing and faithful picture of the lawyers of fifty years past, when he came to the bar, and of some lawyers today. Their ranks are thinning, and it appears highly unlikely that the portraits of their successors will be painted in such warm colors.

CHAPTER SEVEN

THE PARTIES

IN 1961 THE AMERICAN PEOPLE received an astonishing total of take-home pay, after taxes, of 360 billion dollars—one billion dollars a day. Such aggregate wealth is no assurance of universal well-being; Michael Harrington, in *The Other America: Poverty in the United States,* insists that almost 25 percent of our people live in poverty. But even the term "poverty" today suggests our abundance in terms of comparison with what we consider normal economic circumstances. Our affluence is such that many, not just a few, possess more time and money than are necessary for subsistence. The product of excess time and money is, of course, leisure.

Few developing phenomena promise more revolutionary consequences in American life than the rise of a leisure society—not just a leisure class—in a nation traditionally devoted to hard work, thrift and the material success they generate. The intervention of leisure pursuits and products in our system of values will involve more than mere toleration of fun or play; it will mean a radical realignment of the order of importance to be attached to work and to leisure. As we shall see, so massive a shift will require the judicial process, which has the job of supporting and enforcing the activities men value, to fashion new forms and procedures with uncharacteristic speed and extraordinary inventiveness.

The average contemporary no longer works so long and hard that he must utilize his nonworking hours to come up for air after a grueling workday, like an underwater swimmer coming to the surface to relieve his bursting lungs. The periods between working hours, once like a boxer's respites between rounds, are no longer necessary solely to replenish one for the job ahead. They have recently expanded so enormously that they leave many of us unprepared to utilize them advantageously.

Whether leisure time is spent in casting a fishing line or casting a piece of sculpture, whether it be financially nonprofitable, nominally profitable or lavishly profitable, its use is playing an increasingly significant role in our way of life. Leisure is fast developing a world of personal values which will vie in importance with the value-world of business and the professions—and which can no longer be ignored by the law as too fleeting, minimal or esoteric to possess legal values. As Dr. A. T. W. Simeons has said in *Man's Presumptuous Brain:* "Metropolitan man has largely solved the problems of bare existence. He now works mainly for life's cultural adornment— which his brain so insistently demands."

Thus, a generation or two ago, Sundays and the few weekday hours between the close of business and bedtime became to many workers an integrated, essential part of their work week. Some utilized this time in innocuous entertainment or sought spiritual strength to sustain them in the job that always lay ahead. Others drank and caroused in an effort to blot out briefly the dismal prospect of return to work. And some, in true American tradition, studied or dreamed and labored to improve themselves and win promotion to more attractive and remunerative oc-cupations. Only a few, however, enjoyed their leisure as a substantial unit of time and activity separate and apart from their jobs. And so the law, reflecting the viewpoint of the man on the street, recognized no legal or at least compensable value in leisure time.

Two clearly emerging sets of economic conditions underline the onrushing changes that promise an unprecedented and important use of leisure time. One is the drastic diminution in the work week, for the housewife as well as for the wage earner, because of time-saving mechanical devices. The other is the rapidly rising "discretionary" income—that is, the excess over requirements for food, shelter, clothing and other necessities that can be used for additional comforts, better education, speculation or sheer show-ing off through some nonessential channel of ex-penditure elected by the family.

The enormous growth in the American output per man-hour in the last one hundred years most graphically tells the story of the rise of leisure, as we increase our resources while decreasing the time needed to produce those resources. Productivity per man-hour doubled from 1850 to 1900, then almost doubled from 1900 to 1930, and more than doubled still again from 1930 to 1960. Yet another rise of 50 percent is expected for the decade from 1960 to 1970.

The extent to which the worker has benefited from the recognition of his right to leisure time, as evi-denced in social legislation and trade union negotiated contracts, can be shown quickly and dramatically. Prior to 1800 the average work week was 80 hours; by 1900 it was 56 hours; by 1950 it was 40 hours. A survey of metropolitan areas for the year ending June 30, 1960, showed that about 60 percent of all employees in the northeast had regular schedules calling for less than 40 hours per week, usually 35. Pressures are developing to reduce this last figure, and it is not unlikely, in view of the probable effects of automation upon our labor force, that by 1975 the average work week will be 30 hours.

Contributing more literally to the prospect of a leisure society is, in the words of the *Fortune* magazine editors, the startling but likely rise by 1970 of "a vast number of adult Americans, perhaps 25 million, [who] will be 'making a living' without actually working . . ." Even today, 15 percent of all personal income in the United States is derived from activity no more laborious than receiving rents or dividends or clipping interest coupons, cashing social security, life insurance or pension payments. About five and a half million persons over fourteen years of age are engaged neither in work, schooling, housework or any other such activity, and this number was only approximately 2,000,000 just ten years ago. Sylvia Porter, the financial writer, has made the point that "not ever in our economy have so many received so much income without currently working for the income."

Economists have fixed an annual income of roughly $4,000, after taxes, as sufficient to provide the average family unit with the necessities of food, clothing, shelter, transportation and medical care. The excess over that figure provides the so-called "discretionary" income mentioned earlier. The state of our economic well-being in 1960 was disclosed vividly by the fact that the average family income before taxes was $6,900, and more than two-thirds of all families had annual incomes in excess of $4,000. From 1947 through 1960 the average family income rose 67 percent, and *Fortune,* projecting probable economic trends, estimates that by 1970 almost 85 percent of all family units will earn in excess of $4,000 (based upon 1959 dollars), and about twenty-five million family units will have incomes above $7,500 before taxes.

Leisure, in the American sense at least, means money as well as time to spend it. The economy has supplied and promises to continue to supply the wherewithal. Writing of the average city worker, Sylvia Porter has reported that the percentage of income spent for nonnecessities increased from 17 percent in 1901 to 40 percent by 1950, and 44 percent by 1960. The avidity of the American pursuit of leisure is reflected by the doubling of American expenditures on reading since 1950; the doubling of vacation and travel spending since 1947; the rise by almost 150 percent in money spent on television sets, radios, phonographs and records from 1947 to 1958; the two-and-a-half-times increase in money spent for private education since 1947; *the devotion in 1959 to the "fun market" of almost 41 billion dollars out of a total income after taxes of 336 billion dollars.*

Economists seem agreed that Professor Galbraith was not guilty of mislabeling when he termed us an affluent society. From 1950 to 1959 total expenditures in the United States on food, clothing and other personal goods and services rose from $100 billion to $125 billion, and it is suggested by the *Fortune* editors that this figure will rise to $175 billion by 1970. W. W. Rostow sees the great post-World War II boom as a resumption of the boom of the 1920s, resulting in the following decisive indicia of an age of high mass-consumption of machinery for providing fun and saving labor:

> . . . in 1948 54% of American families owned their own cars; a decade later, 73%. In 1946, 69% of houses wired for electricity had electric refrigerators; a decade later the figure was 96%; and the figures for other electric gadgets—for example, the vacuum cleaner and electric washer—are similar. Television was installed in 86% of such homes by 1956.

The attainment of abundance has engaged the attention of all manner of students. Professor Abraham Edel of the City College of New York has discussed brilliantly the ethical and philosophical issues provoked by an economy of abundance; Galbraith, and Robert Theobald in *The Challenge of Abundance,* have given popular currency to the economic and political problems resulting from productive abundance; Professor Arnold Toynbee has considered with sweep and imagination the historical implications of a surfeited society; Professor David Reisman has explored the sociological implications of a productively abundant, consumer-oriented and status-anxious society. In *The Future as History,* Robert L. Heilbroner has reviewed the problems of the nature and disposition of the labor force as automation and other production techniques further increase American abundance; David M. Potter, in his *People of Plenty,* discussed perceptively the historical effect of abundance upon the American character; C. Wright Mills of Columbia used, in many works, a scholarly though polemical technique to update the economics of Marx and Veblen in the light of our current and probable abundance. Professor Rostow has, in part, predicated his widely discussed analysis of the universal stages of economic growth upon our attainment of an age he designates as one of high-mass consumption. Dr. Gardner Murphy's germinal work, *Human Potentialities,* and several of the recent writings of Eric Fromm consider the prospects of human emotional and, indeed, evolutional development from the vantage point of an economy of plenty. This list could be extended considerably, but there has been no comparable discussion of the effect of our abundance upon the law in general or the judicial process in particular.

Many phases of our era of plenty will be reflected in the courts, but none as surely as the historically unique phenomenon of the rise of a leisure society. If the function of law, and especially of the judicial process, is to articulate and protect the recognized values of a society, our affirmation of a heavy premium upon leisure values must and will find its true echo in the judicial process. Reisman anticipates the novelty of the emerging problems when he points out: "Because the distribution of leisure in America has been rapid as well as widespread, leisure presents Americans with issues that are historically new." And so a consideration of some of the legal problems connected with our new leisure is in order, even if, as Reisman also observed, "many people are uncomfortable when discussing leisure: as with sex, they want to make a joke of it."

Judicial accommodation will be required to what we might call personality rights—those rights and interests incidental to a leisure society. Personally satisfying activity, which may be nonproductive in the economic sense, will increase in quantity and importance. The nature of leisure activity may be expected to change from the marking of time between working hours—what Reisman called "a permissive residue left over from the demands of work-time"—to the fulfillment of the individual's unique needs and potentials for expression and satisfaction. If, as Flaubert said, "every notary bears within him the debris of a poet," the leisure society would allow the notary-poet to take pen in hand to draft a deed or to scribble verse; and our courts will have to recognize and protect both endeavors.

The capacity of the courts to transfuse newly developed values into the system of values accorded judicial recognition has been one of the highly vaunted characteristics of our common law process. The adaptive quality of established principles to new situations, as well as to new shadings of old situations, has been the lubricant of our judicial system. English common law helped smooth the massive transition from the feudal society to a free market by protecting freedom to transfer land and, later, personal property; by evolving the devices necessary for the enforcement of rights and obligations arising out of contractual relationships; by extending the concept of property rights from realty to personalty, and to intangibles such as notes, stocks, bonds, etc.; by participating in the development of the trust and later the corporate forms; and by injecting mercantile custom and practice into the mainstream of commercial litigation. The rub is, however, that these great accommodations were made, as law followed history, with a slow majesty completely unsuited to the tempo of our times.

The past century's history of the evolution of the rule of liability for injuries caused by consumer products—such as contaminated canned foods, exploding soda bottles, harmful cosmetics, defective vehicles—illustrates the sure but slow process of the common law.

Before the onset of the Industrial Revolution, most commodities were purchased locally from the person who made them. Meats were bought from butchers who slaughtered the animals themselves and who did not buy from meat packers enjoying a national distribution. Wagons were purchased from the local carriage-maker, not from the local distributor for a national manufacturer. The maker of an article in commerce was far more likely to be the retailer than the manufacturer of today.

Therefore, if someone became ill from tainted foodstuffs, or was injured because of a defective wagon wheel, he did not have to choose whether to sue the seller or the processor or the manufacturer, or all—they were one and the same person. The remedy which slowly developed for the sale of defective goods was legal action for breach of contract by the seller, rather than for negligence on the part of the seller (an entirely different kind of lawsuit, usually more difficult to prove than breach of contract). Every agreement to sell is in essence a contract, written or oral. Most retail sales represent oral contracts; a man purchasing butter or meat or a ladder is not apt to ask for a written contract of sale. To protect the purchaser, the law assumes that every contract of sale, oral or in writing, contains certain warranties which are, in effect, assurances of the quality of the goods sold. If the seller's representations are not expressed in writing—and they seldom are—then they are deemed implicitly made by him nevertheless. They are therefore known as implied warranties.

The implied warranty invoked in a suit for injuries caused by consumer products is that the goods are fit for the use intended—food that is safe to eat, vehicles that are safe to ride in. It is usually quite difficult to prove that a defective condition was caused by negligence in the preparation or manufacture of a product; it is comparatively simple to prove that, irrespective of the defendant's negligence, the defective condition constituted a breach of an implied warranty. Besides, the seller's obligation for breach of warranty is strict and absolute, and does not depend upon proof of negligence. For very practical reasons, therefore, most lawsuits in these cases have been brought for breach of warranty.

It has, however, been a fundamental rule of law that, with some few exceptions, one may sue for breach of warranty only if he is in privity with the one sued—that is, if both are parties to the contract. Obviously, this rule posed no problem when the purchase was made directly from the only party liable for damages instead of, as today, from a retailer who is at the end of an intricate organization distributing the manufacturer's products, with intervening middlemen unknown to the buyer. It is understandable, therefore, why at first there were no well-defined lines of demarcation between actions for breach of warranty or for negligence in this type of case.

It made little difference until 1842, when the leading case of *Winterbottom* v. *Wright* was decided in England. This case has been interpreted as requiring privity of contract in cases for damages—whether based on negligence or breach of warranty—arising out of the use of defective consumer products. The doctrine born of that case, which was decided during the gathering impact of the Industrial Revolution, expressed fear of the consequences to manufacturers in infant but expanding industries if their duty of care extended to remote strangers. It was apprehended that they might be held liable for damages far exceeding the sale prices of their articles, long after the manufacture and sale had been completed.

We can appreciate, a hundred and twenty years later, that this insinuation of privity as a major obstacle to the recovery of damages in negligence suits had its origin in social and economic concerns rather than in legal logic or philosophy. But it is a fundamental rule of law that when a person tolerates a dangerous condition which he should have foreseen could injure the person or property of others, he should be responsible for the consequences of his conduct. As the newly interposed privity requirement frustrated the application of this general principle in case after case in which defendants had been guilty of outrageous negligence, the courts began to squirm into exceptions to the newly pronounced privity rule.

With the passage of years the exceptions multiplied, particularly to relieve the harshness of the privity rule in cases involving the manufacture of inherently dangerous articles when it was inescapable that the manufacturer should have foreseen the prospect of injury to persons purchasing from remote and often financially irresponsible retailers. As the conditions that prompted such judicial paternalism have changed, and its underlying tenets have been proven unsound, the area of the manufacturers' immunity from suit has progressively and perceptibly shrunk. While Chief Judge of the New York Court of Appeals, Justice Cardozo said: "The assault upon the citadel of privity continues these days apace."

As far back as 1852 New York State courts began nibbling away at the frontiers of privity. Recovery was allowed for the negligence of a defendant who had substituted poison for a curative drug, although the manufacturing defendant's dealings were only with the retail druggist who had sold the drug to the plaintiff, and not with the plaintiff. And shortly after the turn of this century the same court permitted a bystander—not the purchaser or user—to recover damages directly from a manufacturer for injuries caused by the explosion of a coffee urn. The inherent character of the urn was such that "it was liable to become a source of great danger to many people if not carefully and properly constructed."

Then, in 1916, came the landmark opinion of the New York Court of Appeals in *MacPherson* v. *Buick Motor Company*, written by Chief Judge Cardozo, which now represents the law in probably every state in the country. It demolished the illogical and impractical rule that lack of privity would immunize a manufacturer against his negligence unless the article was in and of itself inherently and imminently dangerous. The *MacPherson* case imposed liability if the manufacturer's negligence caused the article—in that case a defective automobile wheel—to become a thing of danger no matter how innocent in appearance. The process started by *MacPherson* "continues these days apace," even in the area of implied warranty. Each year has brought evidence of further riddling of the privity rule, all through judicial ingenuity operating within the consistent concepts—albeit sometimes stretched relentlessly—of the common law.

Two cases, typical of the trend, were decided within the past few years at opposite ends of the continent. In New York a child injured her mouth on metal particles in canned food that had been purchased by her father, and sued on the theory of breach of warranty; the Court of Appeals swept away previous judge-made law that forbade recovery in warranty to anyone except the purchaser, by holding that the father's purchase "was made for all the members of the household." And in California the Supreme Court upheld the contention of an injured employee, suing the manufacturer of an abrasive wheel, that he could be considered a member of the industrial "family" of his employer, who had bought the defective wheel.

In 1962, the Court of Appeals, in a case based on express warranty, relaxed the requirement of privity even further. A manufacturer of children's garments purchased goods from a textile company; the textile company had treated the goods with a chemical to prevent shrinkage and had warranted against shrinkage; when the children's clothing shrank in ordinary washing, the clothing manufacturer sued the chemical company, not the textile company with which the manufacturer was "in privity"; the suit was sustained, the court saying:

> . . . The rationale underlying the decisions reject-
> ing the privity requirement is not difficult to see in
> the light of present-day commercial practices. It
> may once have been true that the warranty which
> really induced the sale was an actual term of the
> contract of sale. Today, however, the significant
> warranty, the one which effectively induces the pur-
> chase, is frequently that given by the manufacturer
> through mass advertising and labeling to ultimate
> users or to consumers with whom he has no direct
> contractual relationship.

It is clear that the slow, remorseless judicial process will soon raze the citadel of privity completely. It will, belatedly to be sure, reflect the century-long shift from protecting marginal producers in an era of scarcity to safeguarding consumers unable to protect themselves in an era of abundance. Judicial opinions are repeatedly suggesting that it is economically and socially more defensible to place the burden of the risk on the manufacturer, who can spread, absorb and insure against it and pass the cost along to the consuming public.

You may well ask: why must so patently necessary a job of law revision be done piecemeal? Why can't the highest court in each jurisdiction consider every aspect of this tangle of decisions and take advantage of the first appropriate case that comes along to pronounce a sensible and consistent pattern for all consumer product cases? Or, if the judiciary is not so disposed, why can't the legislature, that powerhouse of lawmaking, supersede all this huffing-and-puffing case law by enacting a comprehensive statute attuned to the times and needs?

The answer is plain. Precedent is the polestar of the law. Judges like to make new law by applying old, established principles to new situations. They would recoil from proceeding as businessmen or professionals in other fields might think appropriate—to survey the entire problem and as legal engineers prepare a blueprint of an entire structure of law. This would smack too much of the legislative process; and judges never like to be accused of poaching on the legislative preserves. Much can be said for such restraint. Among other things, the avoidance of large, sudden, tearing changes makes for predictability and stability, attributes prized by prudent men in ordering their affairs, and regarded as essential by lawyers in order to advise their clients with assurance.

In turn, legislatures are reluctant to revise the common law. Most of them are manned by a majority —or at least a large number—of lawyers, who are wedded to the common law by training as inexorably as the judges. Short sessions and crowded calendars do not permit the time and energy required for the deep consideration that must precede any wholesale revision of existing law. And to refer the matter to a legislative committee for thorough study and report usually means putting it again in the hands of lawyers.

The emergent body of law relating to leisure time will encounter in the courts many difficulties similar to those met in the past by the law relating to consumer products. It too will be called upon to cope with a new and dimly comprehended world of social and economic values. And it too will be torn between remaining within its womb of precedent and recognizing its responsibility to collaborate in this brave new world. But we cannot any longer hope, over the next few generations, to build a wholesome and harmonious body of law for the problems that will arise from the rapid growth of leisure time simply by cementing together cases as they happen to thread their way through the courts, and without preparing plans for constructing a homogeneous structure.

Currently at least, privacy, mobility and freedom to hear and read as well as freedom of expression and association—all basic components of leisure—are safeguarded in many respects against invasion by government. The First Amendment of the United States Constitution, binding by its terms upon the federal government and judicially extended to the states, is the fundamental safeguard for the listed freedoms. The due process clauses of the Fifth and Fourteenth Amendments are also designed to provide further assurances against undue government impairments of the freedom to enjoy leisure values. In sustaining freedom to travel as a constitutionally protected right under the due process clause, United State Supreme Court Justice William O. Douglas has commented that "freedom of movement also has large social values."

But the rights stemming from leisure will not be protected solely by assurances against governmental encroachment. The more substantial problems will arise as leisure activities—or, for that matter, inactivities—collide with traditional property rights or interests. We recall the deference which the courts originally paid the demands of industry when the fumes, dirt and noise incidental to production and transportation invaded homes and entire communities. But as leisure, with its necessary emphasis upon the aesthetic rather than the functional, comes to assume new significance in our society, new balances will have to be struck. Just such readjustments are at the heart of zoning and planning legislation and regulation, for their constitutionality is in part based upon the value attached to aesthetic considerations. So much was indicated by the United States Supreme Court in 1954. In sustaining the validity of a locality's exercise of the zoning power, that court observed:

> . . . The concept of the public welfare is broad and inclusive . . . The values it represents are spiritual as well as physical, aesthetic as well as monetary. It is within the power of the legislature to determine that the community should be beautiful as well as healthy, spacious as well as clean, well-balanced as well as carefully patrolled . . .

Today zoning for beauty is so well accepted that it may be forgotten that the first comprehensive zoning ordinance was not adopted until 1916 in New York City.

No doubt many conflicts between conventional forms of property rights and new leisure values will be negotiated by legislation rather than through adjudication. It will be for legislatures to make the large, hard choices between the privacy and quiet necessary for contemplative leisure pursuits and low-flying aircraft or ear-shattering jets; between noxious industrial fumes and refreshing gardens; between the use of harbors for cargo craft or for pleasure cruisers; between income and entertainment taxes; between the competing demands of industry and of fun for items in short supply.

It will remain for the courts to resolve the particular instances of the impending conflicts between traditional property rights and emerging leisure values, while the legislatures will probably supply the more generalized solutions and accommodations. Not even the most perspicacious of the lawmaking bodies could hope to anticipate all such conflicts. Many legislatures will surely leave a substantial portion of these problems to the judicial process, which has long been engaged in weighing and adjusting competing interests case by case.

Even now each year finds the law books more and more occupied with decisions bearing upon what we have called personality rights. Loss of marriage prospects resulting from an eye injury to a ten-year-old girl were, in 1962, held to be compensable by a jury. In 1960 a riveter suffering from headaches caused by a facial injury was awarded $20,000, the Missouri court saying that "he had to forego such ordinary but fundamental pleasures as playing ball with his boys, joining with them in scout activities and playing pinochle with his wife and their mutual friends." Two recent Pennsylvania opinions sustained awards based upon injuries impairing senses of taste and smell, pointing out that "the loss of the sense of taste is one of the most grievous losses in the keen enjoyment of life." A United States Military Court has just held that an order to a serviceman not to drink liquor was an arbitrary and illegal restriction on the personal rights of the individual, when not shown to be connected with the "morale, discipline and usefulness" of the military service.

A related trend is developing to compensate workers for emotional illnesses sustained in the course of employment that would have been denounced as downright pampering a few years ago. In Michigan, it was held that a worker was entitled to workmen's compensation benefits for disability caused by emotional pressures induced by production-line pressures, although the employment was not unusual and he was not subjected to emotional pressures different from those encountered and resisted successfully by his fellow workers. In many jurisdictions compensation awards have been allowed for some years for psychoneurotic disabilities induced by a single occurrence. In Texas, a claimant ironworker saw a fellow employee plunge to his death, causing him to develop an anxiety reaction which rendered him unable to continue to work as an ironworker. And in Massachusetts a claimant, without physical contact on her part, suffered a paralysis resulting from a conversion reaction when lightning struck the building in which she was working. Both claimants were allowed compensation awards.

The liberal trend evidenced by these and similar rulings has had to overcome an understandable reluctance to award compensation for psychoneurotic disabilities. Not only do these derive from mysterious mental causes, as compared with fractures which can be traced by X ray; but it is often most difficult to present reliable evidence as to the intensity, duration and extent of such injuries. Traditionally the common law has been hostile to claims of injuries which can be easily simulated. But it is not a far cry from recognizing derangement of personality as a compensable injury to accepting the legal values of personality rights.

A comparable development is beginning to emerge with respect to the once impregnable rule of law that allowed recovery for damages suffered in an accident only when there has been a physical impact or blow. At common law, if a horse through negligent handling rears directly in front of a woman and frightens her so badly that she sustains a conversion hysteria, she may not recover; if, on the other hand, the horse's tail gently brushes her person, she is entitled to damages. In one case, decided in Connecticut in 1930, where the plaintiff heard a loud crash and fainted with fright, it was held that the falling of her body to the ground satisfied the requirement of a physical impact.

The prospect of judicial recognition of leisure values is engaging. There is no small irony in the application of our most sedate institution to the protection of the right of fun, to the equation of the frivolous with the judicially serious. Yet, it is in clear view that our courts will provide judicial shelter for recognition of all manner of fun and adult play—the hot-rodder, the jazz fancier, the amateur chef. We may be confident that there will be no loss of judicial dignity in the process of recognizing leisure values, even some now appraised as frivolous. Judicial protection of such values will not divest the courts of dignity, but on the contrary will tend to invest those values with authority and status.

The judicial inclusion of leisure values of privacy, beauty and freedom of reception and expression in the presently well-stocked inventory of legally protectable rights will necessarily raise problems of judicial implementation. That plastic body of jurisprudence known as equity will probably adapt itself to the new challenges more readily than any other branch of the judicial process. This is because the equity system was conceived centuries ago to cope with problems which had defied the common law courts of those days—problems in many respects as baffling and resistant as those discussed in this chapter.

The common law, through the laudable efforts of judges to give it uniformity and predictability, had inhibited itself in a straitjacket of rigid and unyielding rules and precedents. It proved incapable of meeting the shifting and varying demands of a society emerging from feudalism. When the common law was unable, in the view of a disappointed suitor, to afford him palpable justice, he would lay his case before the king—that is, if he were fortunate enough to gain his ear. The king in turn assigned the matter to his chancellor, who was regarded as the keeper of the king's conscience. As the functionary of the king, who was the supreme lawmaker and judicial officer of the land, the chancellor could mold the law to do justice in a particular case.

So many complaints surged upon the chancellor that separate chancery courts were set up to handle them. These were the first equity courts, and with the passage of time they established their own well-defined rules and precedents. These general rules, however, have always retained enough elasticity to fulfill the community's ideas of justice when confronted with new situations constantly arising within a changing society.

We need not strain our imagination to conjure up new forms of relief which equity will undoubtedly devise to protect leisure rights. There will be many such rights which can be recognized under present equity law. The same equity rules now available to protect property rights are ready at hand for application to personality rights. Injunctive relief which now forbids trespassing upon land could just as well forbid trespassing upon leisure time. A threat to the product of leisure activity would be restrained by injunction as readily as a threat to the product of industrial activity. Specific performance, now confined to compelling the performance of contracts involving realty or irreplaceable items of personal property, could as well be available for contracts involving irreplaceable expressions of the personality. In short, as our rights to bowl or to boat come closer in judicial recognition to our rights to sell or to produce, we may expect that the various remedies already devised by equity will be capable of being mustered into immediate service.

On the law side of the courtroom, however, newly created problems will require creative and imaginative thinking. For in law, as distinct from equity, the objective is to compensate in money for losses suffered—not to do something or desist from doing something, but to pay money damages for what a party has done or failed to do in violation of some legal precept. We may, therefore, anticipate difficulty in value-balancing, as well as problems in assessing monetary values to compensate for the impairment of leisure values in a court system conditioned to assessing damages by monetary loss. Traditional standards of market or replacement value may not measure satisfactorily the monetary values for deprivation of the enjoyment of leisure. It is even doubtful whether relief for such loss can be attained adequately by the recovery of money. For example, a person injured in an accident may now recover for his pain and suffering, his expenses and his loss of earnings. How will we compensate him for his loss of leisure values?

The problem may be better seen if we consider an automobile accident involving the traditional John Doe and Richard Roe. Both are salaried salesmen; John is the driver and Richard his passenger. They are en route to Miami Beach, John on business, Richard for his annual paid two-week vacation. John has some samples and other wares in the car; Richard, an amateur painter, has brushes, paints, canvasses and several treasured but unmarketable paintings he has produced. The accident results in damage to the car, two weeks' incapacitation of John and Richard and destruction of John's goods and Richard's art.

As matters now stand, John can recover his loss of two weeks' pay, and full compensation for the monetary damage to his car and goods. Richard, the painter, would be less fortunate. Any medical expense or pain or suffering incurred by him would be a basis for recovery. But, except for the actual cost of the destroyed art materials, the loss of his paintings is not recoverable; and the ruined vacation, since he received pay, is not usually considered a basis for recovery of damages.

It is possible that a jury capable of assessing pain and suffering in dollars and cents is just as capable of restating in money the trauma occasioned by the loss of a nonmarketable but personally valuable leisure product. As leisure activity and products, valuable to the person but not in the market, become increasingly prized and judicially recognized, current concepts of compensation will require reappraisal.

Even now injury to reputation by libel or slander is the subject of monetary recovery, often without reference to any demonstrated monetary loss. In New York, and many other jurisdictions, falsely calling a man a thief or a murderer or uttering any other falsehood which is libelous per se—among other things, a lie which is so devastating to the victim's reputation as to discredit him in the eyes of the community— permits the injured party to recover a money award without any proof of specific monetary damage resulting from the libel. The rationale which allows money to compensate for what cannot be measured in libel and slander suits is broad enough to suggest the prospect of full compensation for injury to valued though unmarketable products.

The legislative and judicial branches both have the authority to mold new law to regulate the burgeoning leisure values of our society, but history indicates it is unlikely that the legislatures will undertake any comprehensive statutory program. This leaves the field mainly to the courts. The common law, given time, has the mind and muscle to cope with the foreseeable problems. A leisure society, however, is being shaped so rapidly that the mind must be sharpened and the reflexes tuned to meet the challenge currently. In the next and last chapter we suggest the machinery to anticipate and meet this challenge.

CHAPTER EIGHT

THE MACHINERY FOR CHANGE

THE FUTURE ENGROSSES US today more than in any other era of history. Tradition, inertia, security are the binds of the past. But more than ever, change—rapid but clear to see—so sets the fashion of our lives that we are irresistibly forced to look ahead. Samuel Lubell describes us as living "in a world that is out of control, under a technology that seems unable to leave anything or anyone alone." The future is everywhere visible in the technology of the present, and the recent rush of literature about "The Future" is full of explicit visions of what is to come. Prediction today is part of our popular science while for the ancients the future was a mystery, penetrable only by mystics, fixed by fate, and to be endured rather than controlled. Votaries of the Delphic oracle no doubt believed they got full value for their sacrificial offerings when told what the future would be, but not what to do about it. Prophets are rarely planners.

The law and, as we have tried to show, its critical function, the trial process, will lie in the direct path of explosive social, scientific and technological change. Yet, while the startling changes discussed in our earlier chapters are upcoming in each component of the trial process, all of the public and most of the profession know little and have thought less of the inevitable impact of such changes upon some of our profoundest values and most cherished myths. We have tried to alert by stating some of the problems concerning the trial process which we see hurtling toward us. The fact that the knowledge necessary to a wise and considered solution of those problems does not lie readily at hand urgently mandates the building of a machinery of law prevision which will permit systematic, timely and authoritative thinking and action in the area of the future we have staked out.

Of course, not all of the emerging patterns in the trial process need occasion alarm. Some could undoubtedly elevate the administration of justice, just as some could lower it. The only ugly specter we have designedly raised is that of runaway judicial obsolescence working havoc in society because bench, bar and public are neither concerned nor aware enough to anticipate future problems before they become present crises. Nor have we exhausted the challenges to the judicial process which may reasonably be expected. Every informed and interested lawyer could supplement the instances cited. But neither lawyer nor judge today can muster the necessary institutional facilities properly to exploit his prescience. Competent, specialized means of assuring periodic and anticipatory appraisal must be provided not only for existing problems affecting the judicial process, but for emerging problems as well.

It is patently inefficient to leave the resolution of future problems solely to the happenstance of the successive lawsuits in which they may arise. In that setting the watchdogs of the law will forever pursue a mechanical rabbit which will always outstrip them.

The strictures imposed by the particular issue in controversy, the limited breadth of inquiry inherent in the judicial process, the uneven caliber of counsel and judges, all militate against exclusive reliance upon the case-by-case decisions.

Courts are bound to decide cases between individuals, and to declare or make the law only as an incident of such decisions. Lawsuits are usually brought to obtain private satisfaction and not to make public law; and most judges are sufficiently humble and busy to confine their labors to the needs of the case at hand. Even the more talented lawyers and judges are, in any one case, limited by the materials of that case, since no legal doctrine is more unshakable than the rule that proof and decision must be materially related to the specific issues of the case. Few judges would permit the trial of a simple suit for damages—where motorist A struck pedestrian B at location C on date D—to become the forum for a comprehensive, generalized review of the ingredients and integrity of the proper rule to be followed in fixing A's liability. Judge, lawyer and jury would be pulled far from the safe shores of competency if they undertook to explore the extent to which liability for negligence promotes careful conduct, or whether standards of negligence evolved to punish the wrongdoer as well as compensate the injured party make sense where insurance is now available to cover wrongdoers ranging from poor drivers to poor lawyers, etc.

The highest appellate court of a jurisdiction can—and, on rare occasion, does—reverse palpably outmoded doctrine. Lord Atkin said that "when these ghosts of the past stand in the path of justice clanking their medieval chains the proper course for the judge is to pass through them undeterred." But explicit rejection of well-settled doctrine is exceptional; it runs against the grain of an institution which enforces rather than creates rights. And few are the instances where the case and the participants supply the occasion or the systematic data necessary for a responsible consideration of all the weights in the scale which will necessarily disturb its balance by change in doctrine. Blackstone put it that the duty of a court is not to "pronounce a new law, but to maintain and expound the old one." Even Holmes, the most enthusiastic disciple of a creative judiciary, was reported by the late Chief Justice Stone as recognizing that "the common law, when it fulfills its mission, is always adopting new principles from life though never quite succeeding in discarding the debris of outworn doctrine."

Private agencies, whether the huge philanthropic foundation or the lonely scholar, while often admirable gadflies, are likewise unsuited as principal means of exploring and anticipating solutions to problems in the law deemed philosophical and speculative merely because they are not immediate. Of course, the foundation and, often, the scholar may possess the time, the multidisciplined competency, the facilities and the latitude of permissible exploration which are institutionally denied to the courts. These characteristics of private researchers are capable of producing great and even sustained projects, such as the codification of various bodies of common law by the American Law Institute and studies of modern aspects of the legal profession by the American Bar Association, as well as the reports of local bar associations and the law school periodicals. But without the benefit of office, even the most able presentation is usually advisory and tentative as the voice of the volunteer, and not the Establishment. The youthful Alexander and not his tutor Aristotle ruled an empire; Thomas More spoke wisely as scholar but with binding effect as chancellor; and Woodrow Wilson as president of the United States could attempt to realize what Woodrow Wilson as president of Princeton could only hypothesize. The point needs no elaboration for those who may have discovered how the alchemy of public office and authority can transform an idea into an achievement.

This is not to denigrate the enormous influence of the germinal works of Holmes, Cardozo, Stone, Brandeis and Dean Pound in the law journals, or the wisdom and guidance supplied by the American Law Institute's codifications of the law, or the work of the bar associations. But what are needed in this area are the responsibility, continuity and regularity of action, as well as the authority, that attend a duly constituted agency of government. The scholar, whose objective is attained in defining the challenge of the future, is not geared to carry such a continuing burden; nor, for all his power and authority, is the judge, who, when he finishes a case with disturbing future implications, must shrug them off to pick up the next set of pleadings.

Nor should the function we are suggesting be referred to the legislature in the first instance. Many of the prospective challenges to the judicial process are not the proper subject for legislation or codification but rather involve rules—and attitudes—to be fashioned by and for courts. In any event, each of those challenges requires initially the kind of study associated with a permanent, scholarly institution which is often a long-term inquiry unsuited to a short legislative session. Cardozo correctly, and without rancor, described legislatures as "viewing with hasty and partial glimpses the things that should be viewed both steadily and whole."

The Law Revision Commission of the State of New York, to which we referred briefly at the beginning of this book, provides a convincing example of what we have in mind. This commission, brought into being by legislation in 1934, was the response to an increasing critical awareness that the judicial process is frequently incapable of uprooting legal anachronisms firmly planted in precedent and that the legislative process, despite reports of occasional *ad hoc* legislative committees, was frequently uninformed and unmoved as to the need for extricating legislation. Giants such as Bentham, Lord Westbury and Lord Haldane in England and Taft, Wigmore and Pound in this country spoke to the necessity of a mechanism for law reform. In 1921 Cardozo delivered his thoughtful and persuasive "Ministry of Justice" address to the Association of the Bar of the City of New York and there proposed the idea and the form on which the New York Law Revision Commission was patterned.

Cardozo's exposition was characteristically graceful yet powerful:

The courts are not helped as they could and ought to be in the adaptation of law to justice. The reason they are not helped is because there is no one whose business it is to give warning that help is needed.

The duty must be cast on some man or group of men to watch the law in action, observe the manner of its functioning, and report the changes needed when function is deranged.

. . . there is need of the detached observer, the skillful and impartial critic, who will view the field in its entirety, and not, as judges view it, in isolated sections.

. . . the task ought not to be left to a number of voluntary committees . . . Recommendations would come with much greater authority, would command more general acquiescence on the part of legislative bodies if those who made them were charged with the responsibilities of office.

Ten years later—not a very long period for ideas to germinate in the law—an official investigation into Cardozo's proposal was undertaken by the Commission on the Administration of Justice in New York State. In January 1934, the report of this group recommended the establishment of the Law Revision Commission "to receive and consider suggestions from judges, justices, public officials, lawyers and the public generally as to defects and anachronisms in law." That same year the Law Revision Commission was set up to sweep away "legal deadwood." Its legislative mandate was "to examine the common law and statutes of the state and current judicial decisions" for signs of obsolescence and to recommend "needed reforms" in order to "modify or eliminate antiquated and inequitable rules of law, and to bring the law of this state, civil and criminal, into harmony with modern conditions."

The composition of the Law Revision Commission also shows the influence of Cardozo. The five appointive members are named by the governor for a term of five years: four must be lawyers, of whom two are required to be members of law school faculties. The chairmen of the Senate and of the Assembly Committees on the Judiciary and Codes are members ex officio. For a governmental body, the Commission has remained an unusually stable entity; in all but three cases, its members have had an average length of service of about ten years, and during its entire existence the Commission has had a single executive secretary and director of research.

About three hundred instances in which the judicial "function is deranged" because of judicially irremediable anomalies in the law have been carefully studied and reported upon by the Commission, and more than 70 percent of the Commission's recommendations for legislation have been enacted into law. Subjects of inquiry by the Commission have included the right to alimony in annulment proceedings; important aspects of the law of perjury; the necessity of advising a defendant in a criminal case of his right to counsel; liability for injuries resulting from fright or shock; and the formalities of a seal or consideration in connection with contracts. The New York experience was followed by the establishment of comparable agencies in California, Ohio, Louisiana, New Jersey and North Carolina; the Commission also influenced the English Law Reform Committee and the New Zealand Law Revision Committee. The late New York Supreme Court Justice Bernard Shientag, shortly after the formation of the Commission, said that "no more far reaching or fundamental action was ever taken in this or any other state, looking toward the more efficient administration of justice"; Judge Stanley Fuld of the New York Court of Appeals said, more than twenty years later, that the Commission had "fully justified the hopes and expectations of its founders."

But the watchtowers so thoughtfully planned by Judge Cardozo more than forty years ago must now be pushed far forward to fulfill the dreams of the architect. We must now anticipate and forestall future problems, and not merely await their arrival. A unit such as the Law Revision Commission, strengthened with auxiliary personnel trained to identify, analyze and advise on converging trends, and expanded in dimension to deal with law prevision as well as law revision, suggests the machinery which could be considered well equipped to respond to future challenges to the judicial process.

In its first annual report the Law Revision Commission indicated that the Commission would be "not only responsive to suggestions which are brought to its attention but is setting itself the task of studying the needs which have not yet become articulate." The Committee has, however, largely confined its investigations to existing, not future problems. It has, furthermore, according to its able executive secretary and director of research, "excluded the questions that are primarily of policy. We have believed that lawyers could contribute most within their own special skill and competence." No doubt such caution was necessary to insure the safe incubation of a radical idea. The resultant success alone makes possible our suggestion that now, almost thirty years after the creation of the Commission, an analogous device can be devoted to canvassing imminent as well as existing problems; and, in the process, bring to bear not only the "special skill and competence" of the lawyer but of other disciplines so that "questions that are primarily of policy" can be reached.

Proof of the feasibility of the suggested extension of the Law Revision Commission's principles will be found in the extraordinary success of the English royal commissions. For 130 years the British have employed *ad hoc* commissions, made up of distinguished and impartial citizens and experts appointed by the Crown, to study and report on pressing social and economic problems before the country.

An old *Punch* verse, "The Royal Commission on Kissing," runs as follows:

> *I never can remember how exactly we began;*
> *But I seem to recollect a case about a*
>   *clergyman;*
> *A mountain was delivered, rather strangely,*
>   *by a mouse;*
> *There were meetings, there were articles*
>   *and questions in the House;*
> *The necessity for action was clear to*
>   *everyone;*
> *But the view was very general that nothing*
>   *could be done;*
> *And the Government courageously decided that*
>   *the Crown*

*Should appoint a score of gentlemen to track
    the trouble down—
Which always takes a long, long time.*

Witty verse aside, most of the great English social reforms have followed royal commission investigations. The 1833 royal commission of inquiry into the system of rotten boroughs resulted in a vivid depiction of decay and corruption, and was followed by the sweeping Municipal Reform Act. Subsequent royal commissions on divorce and matrimonial causes, on lunacy, on trade unions, on the poor laws, on national health insurance, on ecclesiastical discipline, on child labor, on social security, on the press, on capital punishment, on gambling, on taxation of profits and income, on education and on homosexuality indicate the range and significance of the matters committed to the study of royal commissions and influenced by their findings.

Dean William C. Warren of Columbia Law School, in writing of the royal commissions, has pointed out that

> Their dedication and desire to carry out their appointed tasks has become widely known and respected. Thorough investigations have been conducted, although some have taken "a long, long time." Their conclusions and recommendations have received wide publicity in all media of communication, wide interest by the public-at-large, and sufficient influence on the society as a whole.

Today in the United States the important policy decisions needed on issues such as leisure time, the aged, inflation and urban development, to name but a few, are not being given the attention they deserve. They have become embroiled in political pots, under-or-over-cooked, left raw or with their vital juices taken out. The Royal Commission, on the other hand, has emerged as an institution that combines calm investigation with mature interpretation, in an atmosphere detached from partisan political prejudices.

The machinery for change we envision, then, would combine the continuity and permanence of the Law Revision Commission and the uninhibited range of the royal commission, and would add as an organizing principle a concern for future problems likely to confront the trial process. From the Law Revision Commission we would take the concept of public, profession and judiciary watching the law in action in the courts. The Law Revision Commission even now is so placed institutionally that it can regularly, systematically and promptly receive through the judiciary well-informed advance reports from the field, and also detect trends through antennae aimed at other areas. The same judges and other men of law, properly alerted, would ensure ample notice of the advent of trends of change.

From the Law Revision Commission, too, we would adopt the structure of a fixed, executive-appointed personnel, with tenure, and heavily weighted with men trained in the law. From the royal commission we would import the principle of calling into service citizens of the highest stature as well as technicians and social scientists who could insure that all relevant intellectual resources and disciplines, and not just legal skills, would be applied. Such a complement of ability could not, of course, be directed to narrow or limited issues. Quite properly, questions arising in the judicial trial process comparable to the magnitude of the issues which have engaged royal commissions should engage the consideration of the agency we contemplate.

The selection of issues for inquiry could be left to the agency itself. It might be advisable to require that the issues selected be submitted to and approved by the chief justice of the highest appellate court, who could also have the discretion to initiate inquiry by the agency. In this fashion not only would issues be screened and appraised by the chief judicial officer who directly observes the law in action in the courts, but the subsequent findings and reports would have added weight of authority in the judiciary from the circumstance that the inquiry was indorsed or initiated by the chief justice. We look to the reports of such an agency to serve not only as the basis for legislation, where that is in order, but as a reservoir of intelligence to be used by the courts.

Since the agency reports would be addressed to large and fundamental policy questions evoked by the clash between recent change and old values in the judicial process, those reports, authorized by the chief judicial officer and written by men of knowledge, responsibility and status, might well enjoy an acceptance in the courts comparable to that of judicial opinions. An example of such acceptance is to be found in the history of the New York Law Revision Commission. At the instance of the then chief judge of the Court of Appeals, the Commission made a thoughtful review of the question of the right to sue for injuries suffered by an infant in the prenatal state; in 1935 it reported and recommended judicial rejection of the old common law rule denying recovery for such injuries. The Commission did not suggest legislation on the subject, but looked to judicial action. Thereafter, in 1951, the Court of Appeals reversed and rejected the common law rule, and adopted the views of the Law Revision Commission, citing and relying upon the Commission's discussion.

Needless to say, the agency in view would be no supercourt or superlegislature, but an adjunct of the courts and legislature for their use. And the degree of finality or authority accorded its expressions would depend upon their reception by the institution with the power to take action or decision upon the agency's recommendation. Since matters of importance are vested by a democracy in organs of government which are finally responsible and responsive to the people, the acceptance or implementation of the views of the contemplated agency would ultimately rest with the courts, or, in some cases, the legislature.

Much more could be said of the contemplated machinery for change. But this is, hopefully, an exhortation to action and not an exposition of detail. A further list of particulars is unnecessary if our premise is correct, and futile if it is not. The question we have pressed is whether an exigent need exists for machinery to anticipate change in the law. A sufficiently concerned answer in the affirmative will quickly enough provide its working parts.

The lesson of the story of Joseph is that he not only correctly interpreted the signs of the future in the dreams of Pharaoh, but then proceeded, unsolicited, to set out the means of coping with the seven years of famine which were to follow the seven years of plenty. Of course, there was no time margin for error in Joseph's prescience; the future as foreseen left no alternative to action in advance of the crisis. Parables are never wholly safe as parallels, but we venture to conclude that the press of time and change today demands that the law shape an institution, in the image of Joseph, which will scan the future from the vantage point of the present and suggest how we are to deal with what is to come.

ABOUT THE AUTHORS

JUDGE BERNARD BOTEIN *has been a Justice of the Supreme Court of New York since 1953 and Presiding Justice of its Appellate Division since 1958. He is widely recognized as one of the leaders in the United States of the campaign to reform our judicial systems, and as an outstanding philosopher of the law. He is the author of* The Prosecutor *and* Trial Judge.

MURRAY A. GORDON *is a practicing member of the New York bar. He has specialized in constitutional law and has written extensively for law reviews and other legal publications.*